MANAGEMENT STUD

C000003062

Managing Human Resources

Second Edition

Jane Weightman

Institute of Personnel Management

First published in 1990
Reprinted 1990
New Edition 1993

Phototypeset by Intype, London
and printed in Great Britain
by the Cromwell Press, Melksham

British Library Cataloguing in Publication Data
Weightman, Jane
  Managing Human Resources. – 2 Rev. ed. –
  (Management Studies; Series 1)
  I. Title II. Series
  658.3

ISBN 0–85292–520–4

Contents

List of Figures

List of Figures

Editors' Foreword

Today's business environment demands that managers possess a wide range of knowledge, skills and competencies. As well as a sound understanding of management processes and functions, managers need to be able to make the best use of their time and talents, and of other people's, and to work with and through others to achieve corporate objectives. They also need to demonstrate a full understanding of the business environment and of their organization's key resources: its people, finance and information.

Management education in Britain has at last begun to take full account of these business realities. In particular, the Professional Management Foundation Programme is a major initiative developed by a group of forward-looking professional institutes to meet these needs. They recognize that a synthesis of knowledge and skills, and theory and practice, is vital for all managers and those aspiring to management positions.

For many years, the Institute of Personnel Management has been strongly committed to developing professional excellence. This major new series reflects this ideal. It covers five key areas: management processes and functions; the corporate environment; managing human resources; management information systems and statistics; and finance and accounting for managers. In drawing on the expertise of experienced teachers and managers, this series provides all students of management with an invaluable set of practical, introductory and informed texts on contemporary management studies.

MICHAEL ARMSTRONG
DAVID FARNHAM

1

The Core Disciplines in Managing Human Resources

Managing human resources is an extremely important part of making organizations work well. Managing human resources means acknowledging that the humans in the organization are the most important part of getting things done. The human resources approach assumes that no amount of clever work with figures, or the latest technical equipment, will deliver anything unless people agree to work in co-ordination with each other. This applies to everyone in the organization. An alternative view is that of industrial relations writers, who assume that there is basic conflict in the employment relationship. This makes mutual accommodation necessary because the conflicting interests can never be reconciled. Whichever perspective you hold, studying the management of human resources will be useful to you at work. By understanding other people and how they interact you will be able to get things done more easily.

The 1980s have been full of studies showing that the true role of senior management is not worrying about formal planning and figures but working with people. For example, an excellent British study of strategic investment decisions in large diversified companies showed that organizational structure, measurement and reward systems and organizational climate significantly affected the decisions that were taken.[1] This study also showed that managers influenced events in all sorts of informal ways, so that the decisions had often been taken before the formal meeting. Managing human resources needs to account for both the formal and the informal relations between people at work.

To study the management of human resources we need to look at ideas and evidence from several traditions. First there is material which originates in the social sciences: psychology, sociology, political theory and philosophy. These subject areas have developed individual specialisms in work organization. You will find psychologists using the phrase 'organizational psychology' or

1

'organizational behaviour' in the titles of books. Sociologists and political theorists use phrases such as 'organizational analysis' and 'organizational theory'.

Second is material from personnel management. It involves terms such as 'human resources' and 'human resource auditing'. Third is material from employee relations specialists, who also call their subject industrial relations. Examples of material from employee relations are the focus on the collective rather than on individuals, legal aspects of equality and rights generally. A fourth group of material comes from what the Americans call management specialists: ideas, research and practice that are devoid of any academic pedigree but look particularly at work organization from the management perspective.

Other sources of material about managing human resources are the ideas of training and development specialists, which are currently very popular. The orthodoxy is that personnel, or human resources, management is something that from a management point of view embraces training and employee relations. Employee relations are, in fact, the management of industrial relations within the organization. Each of these specialisms has a contribution to make in understanding how to manage people at work.

A very influential academic book is *Images of Organization* by Gareth Morgan.[2] He argues that there are seven quite distinct ways of looking at organizations. (See figure 1.) Each is a different sort of probe into a complex area, and each is appropriate for giving us an insight into some aspect of an organization's working. An organization is all these things at the same time. Only by having a variety of strategies for investigating, or 'reading', the situation can we be effective.

In this book I have taken the view that there are useful insights to be gained from all the contributing disciplines to managing human resources. The manager who has a range of different strategies for analysing them is better able to cope with the variety of situations that occur. But first a brief account of each of the main contributing disciplines.

What is social science?

The two disciplines in social science that are most relevant to managing human resources are psychology and sociology. Other disciplines normally included among the social sciences are eco-

Figure 1

Some ways of looking at organizations

---

1. Organizations as machines
   With • orderly relationships
   　　　• clearly defined parts
   　　　• determined order

2. Organizations as organisms
   With • adapting to the environment
   　　　• life cycles
   　　　• dealing with survival

3. Organizations as cultures
   With • patterns of belief
   　　　• daily rituals
   　　　• own language

4. Organizations as political systems
   With • authority
   　　　• power
   　　　• right to manage or individual rights

5. Organizations as brains
   With • think-tanks
   　　　• strategy formulation
   　　　• corporate planning teams

6. Organizations as psychic prisons
   With • trap of one way of thinking

7. Organizations as instruments of domination
   With • some having influence over others
   　　　• work hazards

Source: Based on G. Morgan, *Images of organization.* Beverly Hills, Cal., Sage Publications, 1986.

nomics, geography and political theory. They are not included in detail in this book. However, the idea of people as economically and politically active is important for understanding organizational life, and is included in discussions about how to get things done throughout the book.

When I introduce myself as a psychologist people usually say something like 'Oh, I'd better be careful, then, as you can read my mind.' Fortunately for us all, this is not true. I cannot read people's minds. Another confusion is that psychology is the same as psychiatry. It is not. Psychiatry is concerned with particular accounts and treatments of people with mental illness. So what is psychology?

Psychology is normally defined as the study of behaviour. It may be animal or human behaviour. This study can include detailed descriptions of particular behaviours—for example, how we learn. It may also include some analysis to try to account for why these behaviours happen in the particular way they do. By looking at underlying structures and hypothesizing about the effects of previous experience and the environment we try to understand questions. Why do people choose to do different things? Why do decisions change? Why does someone reject this course of action when the previous person did not? Psychology usually tries to account for the behaviour of individuals, but that includes what happens to them when they are in groups large or small.

A particular branch of psychology that is relevant to managing human resources is *organizational psychology*. People working in this area apply the findings of psychology to work organizations. They also do research into organizations to try to improve our understanding of them. As with all psychology, there is particular emphasis on the effect on individuals and their effect on others. This includes questions such as: what do managers do? How do groups influence each other? How does change happen most effectively? I use several examples from this branch of psychology in this book. An excellent book, for anyone interested in taking it further is *Introducing Organizational Behaviour* by Smith *et al.*[3]

Sociology is concerned with the social, group and institutional aspects of human society. There is some overlap with all the other social sciences. What distinguishes sociology is a desire to understand the influences and agreed norms of the institutions of society that affect the behaviour of its members. Sociologists look for generic concepts and patterns that can help to explain social activities. They examine questions such as: what are the roles we play? What institutions are most dominant in society? Does the nature of the community affect the individual's choice of career? How do bureaucracies work? What distinguishes the professions from other groups of workers? Are there different sorts of conflict? What are the effects of different cultures?

These enquiries can then be used to analyse specific examples in work settings, such as the role of a senior manager, the profession of accounting, the culture of the Health Service. Of all the social scientists, sociologists are the most interdisciplinary, sharing ideas and insights with economists, geographers, psychologists and political scientists, as well as philosophical and religious writers. This interdisciplinary tradition is useful for analysing and understanding work organizations. The complexity and variety of the analytical tools that we need to make sense of the different aspects of working life are often reflected in one of sociology's concepts. This is particularly so when we try to understand a specific organization as compared with another or the position of a particular group within the organization. For those who are especially interested in this approach I recommend Morgan's book, *Images of Organization*, referred to above.

Social scientists use all sorts of different methods to study behaviour. Some psychologists use biological methods to study the 'biological basis of behaviour' (to use the title of one of the Open University's most successful psychology courses). This sort of study seeks to determine what are the limits of behaviour and what are the inherited components of behaviour. For example, how is memory stored in the brain? Other psychologists use a scientific framework but study behaviour. They set up carefully controlled experiments in the laboratory where everything is kept the same except one thing; any differences in behaviour are then accounted for by the variation in that one factor. As an example, this type of study may tell us about the ability of babies to distinguish their mothers from other people very early on; it may also tell us that any sort of additional attention to people at work improves their productivity on routine tasks.

Yet other psychologists and sociologists study behaviour in its natural setting, trying to use systematic description and analysis to account for the behaviour. This might involve questionnaires, interviews or observation. Examples would be the study of stress in teachers or the behaviour of street gangs in country towns. Sociologists use interviews and observation to collect their data. Sometimes they use outsider, non-participant, observation; on other occasions the study is conducted by a member, as participant observation. Unlike psychologists, they rarely use controlled experiments, preferring to study real situations.

You will notice throughout this book reference being made to some quite old writings. This is for two reasons: first, the academic tradition of referring to original material where possible; second, the current state of social science. The development of any discipline is never even; sometimes there is a rapid increase in knowledge and theory, at other times progress is slower.

The last decade or two has seen a marked change in confidence in psychology and sociology, with an increase in the variety of views about what is really going on. Two areas where there has been most consensus about genuine development in psychology, for example, are physiological psychology, where studies of the brain's mechanisms are increasing our understanding, and developmental psychology, with its analysis of how children develop. In other areas there is rather less sign of new, fundamental, agreed theories. Much of the introspection and self-analysis[4] is probably because the basic description and analysis of behaviour have been done, and psychology and sociology are now looking at higher-order models and integrations. Many psychologists and sociologists are working in applied areas, such as with the mentally ill, in education and with organizations. It is often quite old references to basic research that give the information that is the starting point for today's applications.

What is personnel management?

Personnel work is directed at the employees: finding them, training them, arranging for them to be paid, explaining management's expectations of them and justifying management's actions to them. The personnel function of management is carried on by all managers. In all but the smallest organization it is also partly carried out by specialists. This is to ensure consistency of treatment and to operate systems, such as performance appraisal and job evaluation, which only have value on an organization-wide basis. Personnel specialists are concerned with satisfying employees' work needs and with modifying management policy and actions that might otherwise provoke an unwelcome reaction.

Personnel management is defined by S. Tyson[5] as managing the employment relationship. Tyson suggests that this has led to three types of personnel department. First is the clerk-of-works type, where the department gives administrative support but no involvement in business planning. The principal activities for personnel staff will be recruitment, record-keeping and welfare. The second type is like the contracts manager, concerned to meet each event with a system as part of the policy network. The personnel staff are involved with informal agreements and understandings, and so become part of the political life of the organization. The third type is that of the architect who seeks to build up the organization as a whole. Personnel staff devise explicit policies which affect the corporate plan and have a system of controls integrated between line management and personnel.

Not surprisingly, professional personnel managers prefer to see themselves as architects. For example, the human resource management experts claim expertise in managing change: a crucial area for modern organizations. Human resource accounting is concerned with the value of workers in an organization; the value is expressed in financial terms to impress on top managers the strategic nature of personnel management.

As a line manager your relationship with the personnel function will depend upon its role in the organization. If personnel are 'clerk of works' they will be a source of information and support for quite specific things. If they are the contracts manager or architect sort of personnel department you are much more likely to be discussing, debating and deciding with them how to proceed in particular areas.

Personnel management professionals are currently debating whether to call themselves experts in personnel, human resource management or human resource accounting.[6] Each of these specialisms has a different perspective. As in many areas of management, the vocabulary changes with time. The difficulty is that sometimes it is because of changes of style, at other times because of a change in substance. Distinguishing the two is not always easy till later.

The contribution of personnel literature to this book can be seen most clearly in Part III, where specific aspects of the employment relationship, such as recruitment, training and poor performance, are dealt with. A very useful book in this area, the standard text for personnel students, is that by my colleagues Torrington and Hall.[7] You might also find our more general textbook helpful for more detailed discussion of some of the ideas raised throughout this book.[8]

What are employee relations?

Those who work in employee relations, whether in organizations or in the academic world, are concerned with the balance of influence and power between different sectors of an organization. One model they use distinguishes between those who hold a unitary view of the organization and those who are pluralists. A unitary point of view emphasizes the right of managers to manage and the need for compliance on the part of those who work for them. There is great use of words like 'team', 'leaders' and 'one happy family' by those holding a unitary view. A pluralist view argues that there are several interest groups within an organization, and that devices for dealing with the inevitable conflict between them need to be found. The emphasis here is on representation, legitimacy and sources of power. This second view is the most commonly accepted perspective in large employing organizations and in management writings. A third perspective is the radical one which interprets organizations as being in the interests of the powerful – the managers – at the expense of other members.

A useful outcome of this perspective is an emphasis on the rights of all members of an employing organization. Such things as contracts of employment, health and safety at work, maternity rights, discipline and dismissal procedures, equality of opportunity for people of different gender, race or disability, all arise from an employee relations perspective. Trade union activity became less obvious in the 1980s but the involvement of unions in fighting for, and developing, these rights should not be underestimated. With the increased use of such things as performance-related pay, one could expect an increase in union involvement as rate-fixing and disagreement with one's supervisor become an issue.

The driving force in employee relations is to achieve a 'felt fair' deal for everyone in the organization. This perspective is particularly helpful in managing human resources when devising routines and procedures to deal with such areas as appraisal, selection, training, or dealing with poor performance. Employee relations reminds us to ask, 'Is this fair?' 'Is this in the interest of the individual?' 'What precedents are we setting?' Where large firms are pursuing sophisticated Human Resource Management strategies questions are usually asked about such things as: in whose interest are these? Is the power reasonably equal between the boss and the worker? What are the consequences for other workers?[9]

Management specialists

There are a large number of people working as management specialists. They may variously be consultants, lecturers in Departments of Management in higher education or business schools, and so on. Many would describe themselves as management developers and trainers. In addition there are people who have become famous from their work as managers and others who have done research on managers. Some people of course belong to more than one of these groups. These disparate kinds of professionals have contributed to our understanding of how to manage people, through their writings, their contributions to courses and through working with us at work. Here, of course, I can only include material from their writings.

Many successful managers and leaders have written autobiographies. They try to pass on what, in their experience, they found worked. An excellent example is John Harvey-Jones, formerly chairman of ICI.[10] A second approach is books based on systematic research on managers, for example John Kotter's study of general managers.[11] Another approach is management textbooks. Here assumptions are made about the nature of management work and the books are written to help managers do their work more effectively from that perspective.[12]

Useful ideas or suggestions can come from these management specialists. Often there is a great deal of wisdom in their writings. The difficulty is that they do not always recognize that what works in one situation does not always work elsewhere. It is also important to remember that they are writing from a management perspective. Academically there are now so many people working in this field, from a variety of backgrounds, that there are almost the beginnings of a management discipline within social science.

The responsive organization

So why study material from these different disciplines under the auspices of managing human resources? In a study of top managers in large organizations, the British Institute of Management concluded that in a turbulent, demanding, global market place, business organizations are having to become more flexible and adaptable, more responsive both to their own staff and to customers.[13] These views are not confined to the business world. Those working in public-sector organizations such as schools and hospitals also feel they are living in turbulent times. Current thought suggests the best way of dealing with this is for there to be less hierarchy, fewer procedures, and networks should replace bureaucracies. It means devolving to small groups and teams the responsibilities for decisions, profits and people. The British Institute of Management argue that adaptability, change and learning are important and should be continuous.

In a world in which a company's products, services and technology can be replicated by competitors with increasing speed, there is a growing realization that people can become the most distinctive asset of an organization. This needs to be understood throughout the organization and ensuring that it is must be the responsibility of all managers.

There are several implications if this is true. Employees are likely to be asked to take more control of their own career and development. They will increasingly be rewarded on the basis of output rather than input, their remuneration reflecting value to, rather than position in, the organization. Individuals will have a greater choice of how, when, with whom and where they work. To attract the best, organizations will have to market themselves and include older people and those who want to work part time.

If this is how organizations are developing it becomes increasingly clear that managing human resources is vital. An understanding of individuals, groups and the organization as a whole is important for all who work in organizations, and particularly for managers. How each of us manages his or her relationships with others will reflect who we are, our moral and our political views. Insights from a variety of sources can help us appreciate the choices we are making and in whose interest we are acting.

Summary statements for managers

- The social science disciplines of psychology and sociology provide systematic models which can help in the management of human resources.

- Personnel management literature provides useful insights, from a management point of view, on the employment relationship.
- Employee relations materials remind us to consider the collective views of employees and other views than those of management.
- Management specialists come from a wide range of backgrounds. They often have useful insights into real organizations.

The structure of this book

How are you going to use this book? I have included a brief summary here of the book to help you understand why there are three sections and the difference between them. If you are looking for professional development then you are advised to read through fairly systematically. If, however, you are looking for some help about a specific problem at work then material in the second two parts is most relevant.

Part I looks at some of the research and the models that have been developed to help us understand why we are different from one another. This is the theoretical base for some of the applications dealt with later on. Having theories and models distinguishes the professional manager from others. These models can help to generate unconventional ideas when none of the obvious approaches appears to work. This is when managing becomes both more interesting and more difficult. Chapter 2 examines different ways of interpreting the behaviour of individuals, drawing on the insights of psychologists. Chapter 3 is about how we learn, and the sequences we go through to do so. Chapter 4 is about motivation. Chapter 5 uses sociology to account for why we differ in our attitudes to work.

Part II still has an emphasis on research but now we look specifically at research done in work organizations, to understand how we can best work in groups. Chapter 6 deals with small groups and how they work. Chapter 7 looks at a range of communication situations, from communication between two people to communication within groups and communication across the whole organization. Chapter 8 discusses how individual managers can make most sense of the organization they work in, to get things done.

Part III is less about research and more about the practical issues involved in specific aspects of managing people. Chapter 9 deals with selecting people for work. Chapter 10 is about training. Chapter 11 is about managing performance and chapter 12 is about how to reward performance. The final chapter is about what to do when someone's work is not up to standard.

I assume that most people reading this book are, or aspire to become, managers. This may mean that you manage something, manage people or are paid a management salary as a professional to advise managers. Whichever sort of manager you are, or become, I assume you have management work to do rather than your just wanting to be a manager. For this reason I have included at the end of each chapter two sections where I particularly draw out from the material discussed aspects that are relevant to managing. The material in the chapters can, of course, be used for other purposes as well.

Each chapter has a section headed 'Implications for managers'. This is where I discuss generally some of the points made in the chapter as they might affect your work. In the later chapters it is quite brief, as the whole chapter is about some aspect of managing human resources. There are specific examples and practices elsewhere in the chapters that are about how to do particular things, such as interviewing.

I have also included in each chapter a series of brief 'Summary statements for managers' of the main points in the chapter that may affect your work as a manager. These are intended to act as a reminder and to draw your attention to the practical issues discussed.

References

1 P. MARSH, P. BARWISE, K. THOMAS and R. WENSLEY, *Managing strategic investment decisions in large diversified companies.* London, London Business School, 1988.
2 G. MORGAN, *Images of organization.* Beverly Hills, Cal., Sage Publications, 1986.
3 M. SMITH, J. BECK, C. COOPER, C. COX, D. OTTAWAY and R. TALBOT, *Introducing organizational behaviour.* London, Macmillan, 1982.
4 See, for example, P. KLINE, *Psychology exposed.* London, Routledge, 1989.
5 S. TYSON, 'The management of the personnel function'. *Journal of Management Studies*, 1987, pp. 523–32.
6 See C. DAWSON, 'The moving frontiers of personnel management: human resource management or human resource accounting?' *Per-*

sonnel Review, 18, 3, 1989, pp. 3–12; K. LEGGE, 'Human resource management: a critical analysis', in *New perspectives on human resource management*, ed. J. STOREY. London, Routledge, 1988.

7 D. P. TORRINGTON and L. A. HALL, *Personnel management: a new approach*. Hemel Hempstead, Prentice Hall, 1991.

8 D. P. TORRINGTON, J. B. WEIGHTMAN and K. JOHNS, *Effective management: people and organization*. Hemel Hempstead, Prentice Hall, 1989.

9 A very useful series of booklets on managing employee relations is published by the Advisory Conciliation and Arbitration Service (ACAS) and is available free from their offices throughout the country.

10 J. HARVEY-JONES, *Making it happen: reflections on leadership*. London, Collins, 1988.

11 J. KOTTER, *The general managers*. New York, Free Press, 1982.

12 One I particularly like is C. HANDY, *Understanding organizations*, second edition. Harmondsworth, Penguin Books, 1985.

13 BRITISH INSTITUTE OF MANAGEMENT, *The responsive organisation*. London, BIM, 1989.

PART I
Individual Behaviour

2

Individual Differences and Personality

We often say to ourselves at work such things as 'Why can't I make any sense of Ross?' 'Why isn't Les more predictable?' 'Why can't Pat be more like me?' Imagine what would happen if we really could understand each other all the time, or predict each other's behaviour, or if we were all the same. It would take away a lot of the frustrations of work but it would also remove most of the fascination. It would be like working with robots, predictable but dull. The great delight of being part of the human race is that we are all different. Trying to understand some of these differences can help us to work better with each other in the following, and other, ways. We learn to be more tolerant and so co-operate better. We are able to communicate more effectively and so understand better what others are doing. We know when someone else may be better suited to a particular task because they have specific abilities we do not have. Can we explain why we are so different?

In the popular press we read of people 'being a personality', or of competitions where pretty girls have to 'have a personality' to get through to the finals. At work we talk of people 'having the personality' to carry them through an awkward posting or presentation. Of course we all 'have' a personality and many of us can 'be' a 'personality'; the interest is in the difference between our personalities. What do we mean by personality and what have psychological theories of personality to do with work?

Psychology can help the manager to analyse why people are different and why they have different personalities. This is not just an academic exercise but can help in getting things done. By understanding the differences among those we work with we are more likely to put requests, demands, expectations in a way that is appropriate to them. When we are experiencing difficulties in influencing someone it can be helpful to have a range of analytical models to understand their behaviour and suggest alternative approaches. When we have a difficult piece of information to give those who work for us we can think of different strategies and decide which is most likely to succeed with the particular individual, if we have some understanding of what sort of person they are.

Most managers already do this instinctively. Psychology helps by systematizing the knowledge and suggesting new approaches when you have tried everything else and it has not worked. Understanding and accepting individual differences is important in our everyday work. The details of psychology can be particularly useful where there is a recurring difficulty and we need a new perspective. To use psychological models effectively requires some understanding of the underlying assumptions. Occasionally this chapter may seem rather academic, and you may find yourself asking, 'Do I really need to know this?' Only if we explore these issues will the applications discussed later in the book have any real meaning. It is the difference between common sense and knowing *why* the common sense is appropriate and helpful.

Nature and nurture

One of the continuing debates in philosophy, from Plato onwards, which has been taken up by psychologists this century, has been the relative contribution of our inherited characteristics, nature, and our upbringing, nurture. This is not just an academic issue, but has practical implications in the extent to which we can modify our own or anyone else's behaviour. If our ability to learn language, acquire new skills and adopt different attitudes is all laid down by our inherited characteristics, then how we grow up and whom we work with will not affect it. If, on the other hand, such abilities are influenced by the environment in which we develop it is important to look at what influences we are experiencing and what influence we are having on others. For example, are we allowing everyone the opportunity to develop? If in addition we find that nurture continues into adulthood, with people's behaviour being influenced by their experience, then there are important implications for managing human resources.

Psychologists, sociologists and social anthropologists tend to focus on the effect of environment on the child. This does not mean that they assume the child is infinitely pliable, but they do assume that nurture plays an important part. If we look at some of their models we will see that each of the main psychological theorists operates with a different assumption about human nature. Each of them would have different implications for management, as we discuss later in this chapter. The Freudian model is a conflict model, with an emphasis on how innate anti-social impulses become restrained by society. Piaget's developmental approach (which has become very influential in education circles) is that the unfolding thought processes of the child enable it to make varying sense of its environment, but that same environment in turn affects the child's thought processes. Those who take the most extreme view are the behaviourist psychologists, who see behaviour as being entirely shaped by the environment, witness the following quotation:

> Give me a dozen healthy infants, well formed, and my own specified world to bring them up in and I'll guarantee to take anyone at random and train him to become any type of a specialist I might select—doctor, lawyer, artist, merchant and, yes, beggar-man and thief, regardless of his talents, penchants, tendencies, abilities, vocations, and race of his ancestors.[1]

So what is the present state of play in the debate? There is still a wide variety of views on the relative contribution of nature and nurture, for several reasons. First, there is no agreement about what should be the main focus of study. Should it be internal structures, emotional or cognitive growth, or observable behaviour in response to social pressure? Second, theorists and researchers tend to work within their own field, with its own frame of reference, that is, with one small part, of the whole: the issue is too big for anyone to be involved in it all. The inevitable result is that each researcher is looking to improve, enlarge and prove correct their own particular model. Third, much of the evidence is inconclusive.

To get a flavour of the debate, consider the following controversy. To what extent is intelligence the result of innate, constitutional characteristics and to what extent is it due to environmental factors? If to this you add the question whether ethnic groups vary in intellectual capacity you begin to understand some of the emotional and political context in which this debate can become embroiled. The difficulty of reaching any universally acceptable solution is due to several factors. First, it is difficult to define the phenomenon. In this case, what do we mean by intelligence? Second, there is the difficulty of setting up a suitable experiment or observation. In this case, how could we separate nature and nurture? Third, there are differences over what is an acceptable statistical conclusion. Similar debates continue over the relative contribution of nature and nurture to language development and the differences between men and women.

The implications for managers of this debate are apparent, for example, when the selection of school leavers is taking place. Should we select only those who have proven ability, or do we take those who have lacked opportunities and expect them to learn once we have given them the chances they need?

It is now rare to hear anyone claiming that nature or nurture is wholly responsible for any particular behaviour. It is the interaction between the two that concerns theorists and leads to different models. It is the interaction between our particular set of genes, which are different from everyone else's (unless we have an identical twin), and our particular set of experiences that accounts for why we are all different, including identical twins who will have different experiences. Each of us is different, and everyone we work with is different. It is consequently inappropriate to treat everyone the same, although we need to treat them equally!

Different models of why people differ

We all need to understand other people so that we can make friends, understand our families and influence each other. To do so we need to see things from the other's point of view, an extremely difficult thing to do. One way of understanding more about the nature of individual differences is looking at theories of personality.

In everyday use we tend to use the term 'personality' to describe the impression a particular person makes upon others. It is the differences in our personalities that sum up the difference between you and me. There is no one best theory of personality. The theory, or theories, that seems to account best for our own and other people's behaviour will vary from time to time and from person to person. In other words we are likely to be attracted to theories of personality that fit our own personality! Our view of personality will affect how we interact with people, and it is well worth understanding what that view is, so we can interpret the effect we may have on others and modify it where appropriate.

Some models for understanding that difference are given here, but there are plenty of others. The three main, contrasting, schools of thought on personality are those of the psychoanalysts, the behaviourists and the humanistic psychologists. Although what follows may appear a historical review of theories of personality, these three views are still the most influential in this area. Let us look at each of them in turn and see what insights they can offer on behaviour in organizations.

Psychoanalysis

The *psychoanalysts* are dominated by the theories of Sigmund Freud,[2] developed from his work in Vienna at the beginning of the century. Freud concluded that personality consisted of three separate parts. The 'ego' is made up of the individual drives that focus a person's particular nature. It will make people do different things from those around them and interpret the world differently. The 'superego' is learned from society. It represents the injunctions of parents, school and other important members of society about what is acceptable behaviour and what is not. The superego can have a modifying effect on the ego. This suggests that basic drives are modified by society. The 'id' is that part of the personality consisting of the basic, animal instincts that make us get going and become involved with our surroundings.

Freud argues that personality develops through a series of traumatic stages when these three aspects of personality are in conflict. Trying to get them into some sort of harmony is the business of maturing. The classic stages described by Freud include the following. First, the early period of breast feeding, with its implicit intimacy between mother and child, which leads to anguish when the child is asked to give it up. Second, the anger felt by children over the external control implicit in toilet training. Third, the disapproval demonstrated by society of childhood sexuality. Fourth, the difficulties for all of us in learning to control anger and aggression in socially acceptable ways. Freud argues that these traumas get pushed to the back of the mind but continue to affect our behaviour into adulthood. The most obvious example is what we call a Freudian slip, when we say something with a hidden meaning instead of what we intended. Another is the early experience of severe toilet training, thought to result in an extreme need for order and tidiness in adult life.

As an example of how this model can help in a work environment, let us examine how one person used these insights. N. S. Dickson used Freudian analysis to look at one particular form of work organization, the army.[3] He demonstrates how military life attracts those who like regimentation and orderliness. This he regards as due to their early childhood experiences. With so many people in the military falling into this category there are not enough who can be flexible when the rules, regulations and procedures do not cover a particular circumstance. Dickson maintains that since those with potty training traumas tend to be drawn to military organizations there should be nothing surprising in the fact of military incompetence.

For the last forty years H. J. Eysenck has been a very popular psychologist in Britain with such books as *Know your own IQ*. He is also responsible for the widespread use of the terms 'introverted' and 'extroverted', originally proposed by the Austrian psychiatrist Carl Jung. Eysenck's main suggestion is that we differ in our basic state of arousal, that is, how much stimulation we require to get us going. Those with an 'introverted' personality are naturally highly aroused, so any extra stimulation sends them into a state of anxiety. By contrast 'extroverted' people are in a low state of arousal and consequently need a lot of stimulation to get them going. This distinction suggests that introverted people will seek out quiet activities whereas extroverts will thrive in large, noisy gatherings. Eysenck has proposed that there is a continuum from the most introverted type to the most extroverted.[4] He has also suggested that people differ on a dimension he calls neuroticism. The implication for management is that we should acknowledge these basic differences in our colleagues and try to organize work appropriate to them.

The usefulness of psychoanalytic models for managers is in understanding that there may be deep-seated reasons for apparently strange behaviour. The models are also useful in giving us some basic vocabulary to describe the differences between people. The difficulty for a manager in holding only to a psychoanalytic view of personality is that there is such an emphasis on the early years. This gives the impression that nothing can be done later about people's personality. This can lead to a feeling of hopelessness if someone does not fit in. But much of our everyday understanding of personality has come from Freud and the other psychoanalysts.

Behaviourism

The *behaviourists* are dominated by the work of B. F. Skinner.[5] His main point is that we learn through our experiences and that these experiences affect who and what we become. He explored in minute detail how behaviour is learned. Skinner emphasizes the external control of behaviour. We behave in the way we do because of our history of reinforcement (rewards). For behaviourists, a *stimulus* evokes a *response* from the individual which in turn evokes a reaction that may or may not be *reinforcing* to the individual. Where the response leads to a reinforcing reaction the individual is more likely to respond in that way in the future. For example, if every time we offer to wash up we are given a grateful hug we are more likely to offer again in the future, assuming we like hugs; if we are told we are washing up in the wrong way, at the wrong time, we are unlikely to offer again.

By studying observable behaviour and the effect of different rewards, given at different times, the behaviourists have built up a detailed technology for specific learning. It has proved highly successful in teaching new skills. A lot of computer programs for teaching are based on this 'programmed' learning. The instructions are made as clear as possible, and when the correct response is elicited a reward is given: it may be 'Well done' or something more concrete. The behaviourists have suggested that if we can find which reward, or reinforcement, each individual prefers, learning will take place more effectively. Reward is defined as that which the person will work for. The process of manipulating people's behaviour by adjusting the instructions, task and reward is called 'behaviour modification'.

There are clear implications here for managers. If personality is learned and dependent on the history of reinforcement, then managers can institute a suitable system of rewards to elicit the behaviour that is required to run an organization effectively. The only task is to analyse the desired behaviours and reinforcements, in enough detail and with enough accuracy, for individuals to be motivated. Luthans and Kreitner, among others, develop this idea.[6] They give reinforcement schedules, analysis of behaviour and the training necessary to enable managers to put it into effect. The application of their ideas does seem to improve productivity. The limitation on applying this approach comprehensively is the difficulty of including the idea of intrinsic rewards, emphasized by A. H. Maslow, for example, as we discuss in chapter 4. It also suggests that workers will be entirely dependent on managers getting the analysis right, whereas many work environments need employees to demonstrate some degree of self-control and personal responsibility. There are also ethical issues related to the degree of control and obedience we are prepared to accept at work. Very few of us have difficulty in accepting the use of behaviour modification techniques to teach a mentally handicapped child to feed themselves. But most of us would object to having the same techniques applied to us by a manager with complete control over us at work—assuming, of course, that someone was clever enough to analyse both the task and the reward accurately enough.

Humanistic psychology

Humanistic psychology has been very influential among organizational psychologists. Unlike the other two schools of thought, it is not dominated by one outstanding figure. This school of thought is really about ideals. It is more a description of what 'could' and 'should' be than an analysis of what is. The central belief is that each of us has within ourselves the capacity to develop in a healthy and creative way. The emphasis is on *becoming* an independent, mature, adult who can take responsibility for our own actions. There may be distortions due to the vagaries of parents, school or society, but we can overcome these difficulties if we are prepared to take responsibility for ourselves.

 Maslow is usually seen as the founding father of this school, with his ideas of the 'self-actualizing' personality. By putting his concept of the person who works for themself to see how far their abilities will take them, at the top of his 'hierarchy of needs' Maslow is obviously advocating this as an ideal that we should all aim for.

 C. R. Rogers has also been very influential.[7] He describes a sequence of stages, for adults, in becoming a fully functional person. First is the need to be open to experience and move away from defensiveness. Second is a tendency to live each moment more fully, and now, rather than relating everything to the past.

Third, increasingly the person trusts themselves more, physically, emotionally and mentally. Fourth, the ideal person takes responsibility for themselves and their actions. To go through these stages Rogers advocates using other people as a resource to interact with.

Consultants working in organizations will often be operating from this particular standpoint. The enthusiasm for participation in decision-making, 'ownership' of ideas, autonomous work groups and developing potential all fit in with humanistic psychology. The emphasis in management training on self-development[8] and the choices available to managers[9] are other examples of this approach being used in practice.

One application of this school of thought has become very popular in organizations, the concept of *stress.* For example, M. Smith *et al.* say:

> The complexity of industrial organizational life is a source of stress for managers . . . The mental and physical health effects of job stress are not only disruptive influences on the individual managers, but are also a 'real' cost to the organization, on whom many individuals depend: a cost which is rarely, if ever, seriously considered either in human or financial terms by organizations, but one which they incur in their day-to-day operations.[10]

Smith *et al.* give various categories of stress that can be identified (see figure 2). Only by deciding when and how to intervene, where sources of stress have been identified, can the stress be reduced. The cure is dependent on the diagnosis but usually some increase in openness and trust is advocated, higher degrees of autonomy and self-management being associated with a healthier organization.

The limitation on using humanistic psychology is that not everyone shares the ideals. Given the unproven nature of some of the basic tenets, it can be quite difficult to persuade non-believers of the benefit of trying the proposed changes.

Other theories of personality

One group of theories that has been widely used by people studying organizational behaviour rejects the idea of motivation and single stages in personality development. G. Kelly introduced the idea that each of us constructs his own world.[11] We each see things

Figure 2
Categories of stress

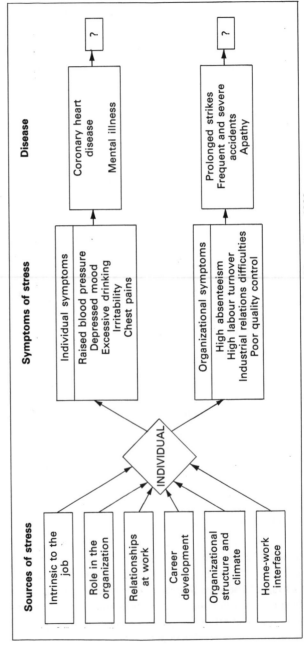

Source: M. Smith *et al., Introducing organizational behaviour.* London, Macmillan, 1982.

differently and interpret things using our own dimensions. This means we each construe the world differently. By enacting many roles and engaging in continuous change we have constantly to practise this process of construction. Kelly's theory is called personal construct theory. Various devices have been developed to discover what 'constructs' each of us is most likely to use.

An example of one such device is the following exercise. Fill in eight different cards with descriptions of things you do at work that are important, time-consuming or frequent. When you have eight, shuffle them and take three at a time. Write down the ways in which two of them are the same and the other is different. Do this with several different groups of three cards. The words you have written down will tell you something about how you construct—that is, make sense of—your work. Another person will have a different set of words.

A related group of concepts are the social learning theories. These deal with the learning of behaviour and particularly the learning of maladaptive behaviour.[12] They emphasize dysfunctional expectancies or self-concepts. Expectancies can be dysfunctional in a variety of ways. If we wrongly expect a painful outcome we are likely to avoid the situation. For example, if you fear that closeness will bring pain, you are likely to act in a hostile way, which leads to rejection by others, which in turn confirms the expectation that closeness will bring pain. Dysfunctional self-evaluation can be exemplified in the person who has no standards of self-reward, so is bored and dependent on external pleasures, it can also be seen in the person who has over-severe standards, leading to self-punishment and depression. All these can be a problem at work. The recommended therapy from this point of view is modelling, guided participation and desensitization.

Implications for managers

The models outlined above are concerned with the overall differences between people. The inevitable conclusion for managers is that they need to be aware of several different theories of personality so that they have a variety of strategies available when they are faced with a situation that needs understanding. We all have a model for understanding others implicit in our personality. This will affect the way we approach others.

E. H. Schein and D. McGregor have both looked at the different models that managers use to categorize the behaviour of their subordinates. Schein gives four separate models that managers use:[13]

- *Rational–economic:* assumes that people are motivated primarily by a rational appraisal of their economic needs.
- *Social:* assumes that people want rewarding relationships at work and are more responsive to group pressures than to management control.
- *Self-actualizing:* sees people as wanting, and able, to be mature, independent and responsible for their own work.
- *Complex:* people vary, and may have any of the above desires, plus others that cannot all be met at work.

As usual, managers are advised to have as many options available as possible and so the last is recommended. You may like to ponder which type you would see yourself as belonging to—and which your friends would assign you to.

McGregor developed a well known model suggesting there are two sets of assumptions managers may hold, which he referred to as Theory X and Theory Y.[14] This is shown in figure 3.

There are many other formal and theoretical models of how and why we differ from each other. There are also the informal models we all have in our heads about what makes people differ one from another. We behave towards other people in line with these beliefs, and expect *them* to respond accordingly. The problem is, they may have quite a different model in their head! Those who know what kind of model they are working with are more likely to recognize when they are using it, and to be aware that others may be using a different model, so reducing the possibility of talking at cross-purposes.

Perception

Another useful concept in trying to understand individual differences is what psychologists call perception. This is the term used to describe the process of selecting, organizing and interpreting incoming stimuli. We all do it differently and so perceive a different 'real' world. To most people it seems ridiculous to discuss the

Figure 3
McGregor's theory X and theory Y

Theory X
1. The average human being has an inherent dislike of work and will avoid it if he can.
2. Because of the human characteristic dislike of work, most people must be coerced, controlled, directed, threatened with punishment, to get them to put forth adequate effort towards the achievement of organizational objectives.
3. The average human being prefers to be directed, wishes to avoid responsibility, has relatively little ambition, wants security above all.

Theory Y
1. The expenditure of physical and mental effort is as natural as play or rest.
2. External control and the threat of punishment are not the only means of bringing about effort towards organizational objectives. People will exercise self-direction and self-control in the service of objectives to which they are committed.
3. Commitment to objectives is a function of the rewards associated with their achievement.
4. The average human being learns, under proper conditions, not only to accept but to seek responsibility.
5. The capacity to exercise a relatively high degree of imagination, ingenuity and creativity in the solution of organizational problems is widely, not narrowly, distributed in the population.
6. Under the condition of modern industrial life, the intellectual potentialities of the average human being are only partially utilized.

Source: D. McGregor, *The human side of enterprise*. New York, McGraw Hill, 1960, pp. 47–8.

way one perceives the world, because the 'real' world is so familiar and stable. In fact the familiarity and stability are to do with our own mental processes, as the actual visual or other sensory input is constantly changing. This section looks at some of the reasons why people may perceive the same situation differently.

First is the obvious difference in *physical sensitivity*. Human organs are only sensitive to a limited range of things. For example, none of us can see x-rays. Some people are more or less sensitive than others—for example, partial sight or hearing makes a difference to the stimulus received.

Second, we have *selective attention.* We notice some things but not others. For example, at a party we can concentrate on one conversation and ignore others; we focus on what is important to us. If, however, someone mentions our name we usually hear it, even in a conversation we are not part of.

Third, we *categorize the* cues as they come in. The incoming stimulation is fitted to one of our existing schemata. 'Schemata' are the categories we have, made up of concepts, ideas and associations built up in our memory as a result of experience. This process may well be influenced by language. For example, in a classic experiment a series of neutral cards were shown to people, each with a different word on it. When they were asked to draw a card, people were influenced by the word they were given, suggesting they had perceived it differently (see figure 4).

Fourth, there is a *limit* to how much we can categorize at any one time. The limit is set not just by how much is coming in but also by the ease with which we can categorize the stimulation. The time we feel most overwhelmed at work is when lots of difficult communications are coming to us. The office party, when there are probably just as many communications but it is easier to categorize them and decide what action is required, is nothing like as daunting.

Fifth, *context* and *expectation* often determine the kind of categorization we apply. If we are expecting to see our colleague at the airport it is surprising how often we misidentify someone else before we meet the right person. Whereas if we meet the same colleague accidentally in the supermarket it may take us a little while to remember their name.

Sixth, our *attitudes* and *personality* will influence what we perceive. They generate expectations. A prejudiced person sees the behaviour of those they are prejudiced against in a negative way, whatever actually happens. A friendly act will be seen as false, a casual approach as sloppy, a remote stance as difficult, and so on. This in turn will affect the behaviour of the perceiver and you get the beginnings of a vicious circle.

The act of perceiving is a constructive process where we make sense of our environment by trying to make it fit our experience. The real world is different for each of us, since we perceive it differently.

Figure 4
The effect of words on perception

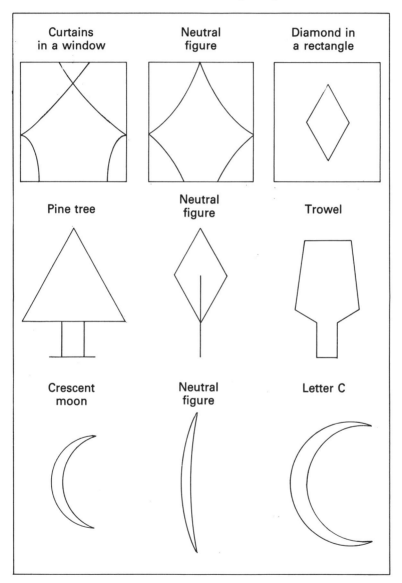

Source: H. J. Eysenck, *The measurement of personality*. Lancaster, MTP Press, 1976.

Implications for managers

This chapter has reviewed at some length the main psychological models and concepts that try to account for individual differences and why we have individual personalities. It is important to remember at work that people are motivated in different ways because they perceive the situation differently. *My* understanding of what needs to be done, how to do it and what I expect out of it is likely to be different from *yours*. *How* different will be due to the differences in our nature and past experience. By understanding and tolerating these differences we are more likely to get a co-operative, productive effort from all those we come in contact with. This does not mean, however, that we have to understand and tolerate *all* behaviour. We try to influence people to be different. Otherwise, as Mme de Stael wrote in 1807, 'To be totally understanding makes one very indulgent.'

Summary statements for managers

- We are all different because of differences in our inherited genes (nature), and our experiences (nurture). Acknowledging this allows us to appreciate individual differences.
- Psychoanalytic models remind us that some behaviour is due to deep-seated conflicts between desires and socially accepted behaviour.
- Behaviourist models give us a technology for human learning.
- Humanistic psychology advocates that mature adults can be trusted to take responsibility.
- We all have different models in our minds to explain why people behave in the way they do. Understanding what these models are can help us to appreciate another's point of view.
- The differences in how we each perceive the world can be accounted for in six different ways.

References

1 J. B. WATSON, *Behaviourism.* Chicago, University of Chicago Press, 1924, p. 104.
2 See S. FREUD, *Two short accounts of psychoanalysis.* Harmondsworth, Penguin Books, 1962.
3 N. S. DICKSON, *The psychology of military incompetence.* London, Jonathan Cape, 1976.
4 H. J. EYSENCK, *The measurement of personality.* Lancaster, MTP Press, 1976.
5 B. F. SKINNER, *Science and human behavior.* New York, Macmillan Free Press, 1953.
6 F. LUTHANS and R. KREITNER, *Organizational behavior modification.* Glenville, Ill., Scott Foresman, 1975.
7 C. R. ROGERS, *On becoming a person.* London, Constable, 1967.
8 M. PEDLER, J. BURGOYNE and T. BOYDELL, *A manager's guide to self-development,* second edition. Maidenhead, McGraw-Hill, 1986.
9 R. STEWART, *Choices for managers.* Maidenhead, McGraw-Hill, 1982.
10 M. SMITH, J. BECK, C. COOPER, C. COX, D. OTTAWAY and R. TALBOT, *Introducing organizational behaviour.* London, Macmillan, 1982, p. 72.
11 G. KELLY, *The psychology of personal constructs.* New York, Norton, 1955.
12 See, for example, A. BANDURA, *Social learning theory.* Hemel Hempstead, Prentice Hall, 1977.
13 E. H. SCHEIN, *Organizational psychology,* third edition. Englewood Cliffs, N. J., Prentice Hall, 1980.
14 D. MCGREGOR, *The human side of enterprise.* New York, McGraw-Hill, 1960.

3

The Learning Process

In order to counter complacency and inertia, management specialists have been vigorously advocating innovation and change in organizations. It seems to have been going on for ever, but it has been especially true in the past decade. Where change is involved, so is learning. It may be a new skill we have to acquire, such as word-processing or a new telephone system. We may have to get to know new people when their company and ours are amalgamated. Perhaps we have to learn the details of the new organization structure so that we can follow the correct procedure for informing people about a forthcoming meeting. Whatever changes are happening, they all require us to learn something.

Another important aspect of learning in organizations is experience. Experience is a crucial part of authority, expertise and effective work. It may be the gradual learning of better ways of getting things done that someone who has been in a post some time takes for granted and is often overlooked when jobs are being reorganized. It may be systematically setting out to learn a different way of doing something such as going on a course or to a conference. It may involve being coached by someone else to improve already reasonably competent behaviour, for example chairing meetings. Experience involves learning.

All these examples of different kinds of learning involve a change in knowledge, skills or attitude. Change can come about through formal training, dealt with in Part III, or by informal processes. For learning to take place the learner must be motivated by the particular learning context.

Types of learning

How people learn has attracted a good deal of attention, not only from schoolteachers but also from people involved in adult training. Traditionally a distinction is drawn between cognitive

34

Info Processing

(intellectual) learning, learning skills and developing attitudes. Each of these is thought to be not only a different objective but also to require a different learning process. The distinction has been refined for practical use in adult learning by the Industrial Training Research Unit. They took the work of the Belbins to develop the CRAMP taxonomy.[1] CRAMP divides learning into five types:

1 *Comprehension.* This involves learning theoretical subject matter. It is knowing how, why and when things happen. This type of learning is best done through methods that treat the whole subject as an entity, rather than splitting it up into bits and taking one at a time. An example would be mathematics.

2 *Reflex learning.* This is acquiring skilled movements or perceptual abilities. As well as knowing what to do, speed and co-ordination are at a premium. This requires practice and constant repetition. An example would be machining, inspection or typing.

3 *Attitude development.* This enables people to change their attitudes and social skills. It is perhaps the most difficult sort of learning to achieve. Group methods that centre on the people knowing themselves seem the most effective as attitudes are very difficult to influence in other ways. One example would be a management leadership course.

4 *Memory training.* This is learning information by heart. It is very similar to reflex learning, where each bit is taken one at a time. Obvious examples are actors learning their lines in a play or medical students learning the names of the bones in the body.

5 *Procedural learning* is similar to memory training but the items do not need to be memorized, only understood and their location known. This requires less practice. Examples are a lawyer's knowledge of the statutes or an engineer's knowledge of how to shut the plant down for maintenance. Neither would need to know by heart what to do, but both would need to know where to look and to understand what they found.

In practice most learning situations require more than one of these types, but the categorization is a helpful means of sorting out which would be the most appropriate way to learn something. For example, in professional exams there are some things that need to be learned by heart, other ideas that one needs to have some understanding of and yet others where procedural learning would be most appropriate. The most effective learners are those who can classify their needs and do not waste time memorizing everything.

How people learn

Before we can start learning systematically, or help someone else to, it can be helpful to know *how* people learn. It might enable us to reduce the time taken to learn something; where difficulties arise, we can start analysing where the problem lies and so do something about it. R. M. Gagne has identified a chain of eight events that occur whichever sort of learning is taking place.[2]

1 *Motivation.* The learner has to want to learn, and want to learn this particular thing or the final product of this type of learning. For example, a professional management student may be highly motivated to become an accountant or purchasing manager and so is motivated to learn about managing human resources.

2 *Perception.* The matter to be learned has to be distinguished from others. This involves identifying a clear objective. At first it is difficult, because one has not yet learned the different categories in the area. With time one learns more and more detailed ways of classifying the matter to be learned. The professional management student at first will wonder how to start and what it is essential to learn. After six months many of the terms become familiar, and identifiable topics that need learning become clear.

3 *Acquisition.* What has to be learned is related to the familiar, so that it makes sense. For example, in this book I have tried to give examples from work settings to help make sense of a new area of study. You can help yourself by recalling your own examples from your own experience.

4 *Retention.* The two-stage process of human learning comprises, first, short-term memory, where items are stored before being transferred permanently to the long-term memory. Not everything needs to go to the long-term memory. For example, the anecdotes and jokes that aid the process of understanding at the time do not need to go to the long-term memory.

5 *Recall.* This is the ability to summon things up from memory when required. There are different levels. *Recognition* is where we know we have seen the item before, and it takes less time to familiarize ourselves with it, but we could not have relied on memory alone. *Recall* is where we can generate the memory of our own accord. You may recognize some of the material in this book as vaguely familiar: it may just seem 'common sense'. Some other bits you could recall from memory without the book because you have learnt it more thoroughly.

Figure 5
Kolb's experiential learning model

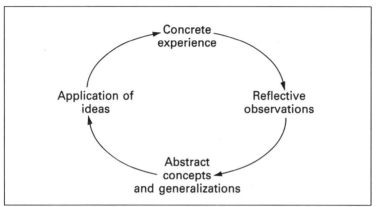

Concrete experience

Reflective observations

Abstract concepts and generalizations

Application of ideas

Source: D. A. Kolb *et al.*, *Organizational psychology*, Englewood Cliffs, N.J., Prentice Hall, 1974.

6 *Generalization*. This is the ability to apply the learning in situations other than the specific one in which it was learned. For example, learning about motivation on this course as it applies to work may be generalized to thinking about motivation at the sports club or in the family.

7 *Performance*. This is where what has been learned is done. It is the test of the learning. The professional management student takes the exam, writes the essay or tries to use the materials from the course at work.

8 *Feedback on performance*. This is where the learner finds out whether the performance has been satisfactory or not. Sometimes it will be obvious because of the quality of the performance, particularly with physical skill learning. But some feedback from the coach or trainer can help to distinguish more subtle levels of satisfaction or analyse what went wrong, how it could be avoided, what needs more practice, what to do next, and so on.

Learning can fail because of problems at any of these stages. The careful trainer or coach will run through this list when helping another prepare for learning and when giving feedback at the end of the learning experience.

Another useful model of learning is that of Kolb *et al*. Figure 5 shows their experiential learning model. All the stages are necessary if learning is to take place. They suggest that the learning process is a cycle of the following stages:[3]

- *Concrete experience.* For example, getting a junior to write a report.
- *Observation and reflective analysis of the experience.* This is most useful if done from many perspectives: in our example, discussing the way the report was written with the boss.
- *Generalization on the basis of experience.* These generalizations use abstract concepts to integrate the observations into the theories we all have about the world. For example, discussing with others how they would handle report-writing.
- *Experimentation in future action based on the generalization.* The application of ideas requires active experimentation. Discuss with the boss possible future action when writing reports.
- *New experience derived from this experimentation.* In our example, getting the junior to write another report.
- *Initiation of new learning cycle.*

This is a particularly useful model for devising coaching and learning experience on the job. See chapter 9 for further discussion of learning and training.

Techniques of learning

Trainers often spend considerable time anguishing over what method to use on a training programme. In Britain the Training Agency spent a great deal of money in schools, colleges, universities and other organizations developing particular methods of training. Such activity can become something of an obsession with process, at the expense of content. In the past there was probably too much emphasis on *what* we learn; now there is probably too much on *how* we learn. Clearly, we need to consider both. When a small group of sixty-four students who were taught in different ways were tested immediately after the session and a month later, there was no difference in the amount learnt through lectures, case studies, role play or other experiential methods. Gale *et al.* conclude, 'It appears trainees can learn effectively in a variety of different modes, perhaps indeed finding as much or more satisfaction from what they are learning than the way in which they are trained.'⁴ This suggests that we should not become too obsessed with how we learn: it is much more important that what we learn is appropriate. Whatever the content, however, there are some general guidelines as to which methods of learning are easier.

We can look at each of the types of learning mentioned earlier under the CRAMP list and see typical ways of training for them.

Comprehension. This is usually achieved by lecture, seminar, discussion or film and video. All these allow the entire theory or argument to be presented together so that it can be seen as a cohesive whole. Clarity of presentation is critical, so that the main points are distinguished from the supporting evidence. Video Arts films are excellent examples of this sort of presentation. The advice of Video Arts (in an excellent video) on making a presentation is to consider the following:

- *Preparation*
  - Why are you making this presentation?
  - What are you going to say?
  - Who are you saying it to?
  - Where will you be saying it?
  - How will you say it?
- *The structure*
  - Preface.
  - Position.
  - Problem.
  - Possibilities.
  - Proposal.
  - Postscript.
  - This plan can also be useful for writing essays!
- *The technique*
  - Delivery: beware mumbling, hesitancy, gabbling, catch-phrases, poor eye contact, mannerisms and dropping voice.
  - Language: use short words and sentences.
  - Visuals: for explanation and persuasion.
  - Detail: better too little than too much.
  - Feedback: ask them.

Reflex. This type of learning is best approached by breaking the task into small steps and simplifying each step so that it can be easily learned. Even a simple piece of behaviour is actually very complicated. Breaking a task down into smaller steps is called 'task analysis'. If we get the smaller steps right we have an opportunity to reward successful behaviour, if the steps are too large there is no opportunity for reward and so learning is unlikely to take place readily. In task analysis we first need to describe the target behaviour exactly. Then we describe the steps that lead to it. For example, when we buy a new piece of equipment the instructions on how to use it are often based on task analysis. The handbook for my word-processor starts with 'Your first twenty minutes'. This section was crucial when I first got the machine, but I no longer need to look at those particular pages. At least some learning has taken place!

Attitude. Learning attitudes is done throughout life and it is very difficult to set out systematically to change them. Experiential methods are usually advocated for this type of learning. They might include some sort of game or exercise that gets the whole group doing something together, for example building a festival tower out of straws that is then judged on height, stability and aesthetic appeal. Or it might be getting the 'treasure' out of a tree with only a piece of rope and a plank. After the 'experience' the discussion is led by a trainer to enable the participants to understand their behaviour better and the attitudes that drive that behaviour. Through such self-knowledge, it is hoped, they will be in a better position to change their behaviour.

Memory. All sorts of jingles and mnemonics can be helpful here. The very use of such mnemonics as CRAMP is an example of their frequent use in student texts. We all try to put unknown things into an order that we can memorize. One technique of memorizing things is to associate them with a ridiculous known sequence, for example learning the shopping list by identifying it with a room of the house. The items are not only identified with the house but seen in it, so that the mental picture is of a dozen eggs in the bath, cereal on the settee and bread on the bed.[5]

Procedural. This is usually learnt through a series of routines. For example, learning how to use the reference system in an academic library usually starts with a demonstration from one of the library staff, then you are given a leaflet with the rules on it, and this needs to be followed by some practice. When you try to use another academic library you know more or less what to do but you need to find out the specific rules that apply to its reference system.

Varied. Assignments, distance learning, self-development

materials and action learning are all methods that have been designed to help in this area. All of them focus on what the learner knows is needed, instead of what someone else believes should be done. It may involve some sort of project work such as that described by Revans as early as 1971, who suggested it as a way of developing managers.[6] Or it may be a series of self-analysis materials such as those developed by Pedler *et al.*[7]

Implications for managers

This chapter has been about the general principles of effective learning. Chapter 11, on managing performance and chapter 10, which has a section on training, show how they can be applied in work organizations. The very fact that three of this book's thirteen chapters deal with this area shows how important change and learning are in contemporary work organizations.

Summary statements for managers

- Depending on the type of learning involved, we need to use different techniques to learn.
- The sequence of learning is the same whatever type of learning is taking place.

Study skills

As this chapter is about learning, it seems appropriate to add a few comments on study skills to assist the learning you are embarked upon as a student of professional management. This will be familiar to many of you. If, however, it is a while since you last studied, or your studying was in a different field, you may find something here to help you.

First, what about reading? While we are reading other people's work we need to ask constantly, 'Is that statement supported by some sort of evidence?' It might be an example, a reference to someone else's work or with some insightful comment. Academically the reference to empirical—that is, systematically collected—

research is always the most powerful argument. We also need to ask, 'How does this fit in with the other things I know about this?'

Second, another aspect of studying is having to contribute something, such as writing an essay, tackling a project or taking part in a simulation exercise. Again, we need to ask, what is the evidence for saying something? How can I integrate my knowledge into some sort of pattern? Would the structure suggested above headed 'Comprehension' help me organize my thoughts?

Third, whilst studying we need to acquire and use several skills. They can be classified in the following way.

Words
- Dictionary: for definitions, abbreviations, quotations, pronunciations.
- Definitions: compare different ones to find the most useful.
- Special use: words used in a particular sense by a profession or by a particular writer.
- Own use: compile a glossary and your own definitions.

Reading and writing
- Selection: use title, chapter headings, contents list and index to select books, chapters and passages. You do not need to read everything in a book.
- Reading speed: select scanning, skimming, or intensive reading at different times.
- Notes: Paraphrase, summarize, select significant quotations as you go along.
- Synthesize: compare different books and your existing knowledge and experience and present the results in discussion or essays.

Evaluation
- Refer statements to original material.
- Analyse arguments that lead to conclusions to see whether there are alternatives.
- Recognize bias, propaganda and the values underlying all statements.
- Accept that there is no single right answer.

Perhaps the greatest asset in studying is a supportive environment. This includes the active approval of those with whom one shares one's life. Many a student has dropped out because there was not enough commitment from spouse or family to allow the time, space or peace to get on with it. It is worth spending some time working to get that commitment if it is not already there. You may find it helpful to look at a book on how to study. There are almost literally hundreds, published by well known publishers such as Penguin, Pan, the National Extension College or the Open University. You will find copies in your local library or bookshop.

References

1 INDUSTRIAL TRAINING RESEARCH UNIT, *Choose an effective style: a self-instructional approach to the teaching of skills.* Cambridge, ITRU, 1976; E. and R. M. BELBIN, *Problems in adult retraining.* London, Heinemann, 1972.

2 R. M. GAGNE, *Essentials of learning for instruction.* New York, Holt Rinehart & Winston, 1975.

3 D. A. KOLB, I. M. RUBIN and J. M. MCINTYRE, *Organizational psychology: an experimental approach.* Englewood Cliffs, N. J., Prentice Hall, 1974.

4 J. GALE, H. DAS and R. MINER, 'Training methods compared', *Leadership and Organization Behaviour Journal*, vol. 3, no. 3, 1982, pp. 13–17.

5 An excellent book about memory and how to improve it is TONY BUZAN, *How to make the most of your mind.* London, Colt Books, 1977.

6 R. W. REVANS, *Developing effective managers.* London, Longman, 1971.

7 M. PEDLER, J. BURGOYNE and T. BOYDELL, *A manager's guide to self-development*, second edition. Maidenhead, McGraw-Hill, 1986.

4

Motivation

In common parlance we often say things like 'Suzy is motivated by money' or 'John is really stimulated by competition'. The assumption is that we can measure motivation. The reality, of course, is that we can only hypothesize that someone is motivated by some particular thing by looking at their behaviour and seeing if there is anything different when the particular 'thing' is involved. Motivation is not something we can feel, smell, hear or see; we can only see the consequences of someone's inner motivation.

We use the words 'motivation', 'wants', 'needs' and 'motives' very freely both at work and elsewhere. We talk of John having the motivation to get on. We talk to Susie about wanting promotion. We listen when David says he needs the project. We discuss with Jean other people's motives for doing things. All these attributes have to be deduced from their behaviour. We are guessing what people are motivated by from how they react in different circumstances. There seems little doubt that, beyond the very basic needs of food, shelter and safety, our other wants are culturally determined. How stable these are, how varied and whether they can be influenced is really too theoretical for discussion here. But as an indication of how some of the studies are put to practical use, other than in management, one need only consider their application in the sophisticated life-style distinctions exploited by advertising agencies, marketing people and the retail industry.

Theories of motivation

Psychologists have studied the behaviour of animals and humans to try to find out what things people will work for—what gives pleasure and what inhibits behaviour. There have been very precise and detailed studies of animals learning new skills, and of the difference that a suitable reward can make. The word 'motivation' is used technically in these studies to describe the hidden inner

Figure 6
Maslow's theory of motivation

Maslow grouped needs into five stages and contended that only
when the needs in the lower stages were satisfied did the next
stage become potent. Once a need was satisfied it was no longer a
motivation although it could return later.

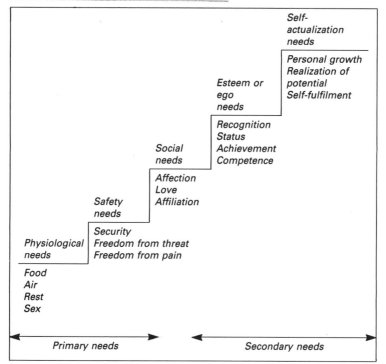

drive or need to seek that reward. Different models have been
developed to account for the variation in motivation across time
with the same person and between different people. The most
famous of these models is that of A. H. Maslow.[1] (See figure 6.)

Maslow grouped needs into a hierarchy of five stages: physiological, safety, social, esteem and self-actualization. The first two of
these he calls *primary* needs: they are concerned with our basic
physical requirements. The other three stages he calls *secondary*

needs; they are learned, psychological needs. He argues that only when need at the lower stages has been satisfied does the next stage begin to motivate. For example, if we are hungry or physically exhausted we are less concerned about being free from pain or secure. However, once we have eaten or rested we will look around to make sure we are safe. He also points out that once a primary need is satisfied it loses its potency, although it may well return later. So in our example the very hungry or exhausted person, once rested or fed, will not then be motivated by food or rest and will be more motivated by the need to make sure they are safe.

At work most of us are free from primary needs, so managers are mostly concerned with secondary needs. Here social contact to relieve a tedious task can be helpful. For example, in one head office where notices had to go out to 20,000 pensioners the manager in charge decided that the whole department, including himself, should spend the last half-hour of the day, for a week, putting the papers in the envelopes as they sat round a big table. The task was done efficiently, as they were all motivated by doing the job together. Esteem needs are met at work through all sorts of status distinctions, for example size of room or company car, having a secretary all to oneself or not, use of telephones for overseas calls or not. Many organizations are now trying to remove some of these distinctions, for instance by having only one dining room or only one sort of uniform. This is usually to reduce the number of spurious status symbols rather than to remove symbols of esteem altogether. *Self-actualization* is the term applied to a person who is motivated by the urge to self-fulfilment, that is, trying to become everything that they have the potential to become. The idea is developed by the humanistic psychologists, as described in Chapter 2. There is some individual variation in the degree to which self-actualization is a motivator, as, along with the other secondary needs, it is a learnt need.

F. Herzberg developed Maslow's model with particular reference to people at work.[2] (See figure 7.) He described the lower-order needs as being potential dissatisfiers if they are not met, but, once they have been, more of them will not increase motivation. This he called the 'hygiene factor'. If managers do not get them right people are demotivated; if they are right no one really notices them, but they cannot motivate above a basic level. In just the same way a hygienic kitchen is not commented on but an

Figure 7
Herzberg's theory of motivation

Herzberg developed his hierarchy as it affects the motivation of people at work. Hygiene factors lead to dissatisfaction if they are not up to standard, but increases above this do not give more satisfaction. In contrast the satisfiers can motivate beyond the basic level, as people want more of them regardless of how much they already have.

Hygiene factors	Satisfiers
Company policy and administration	
Supervision	Achievement
Working conditions	Recognition
Salary	Work itself
Relationship with peers	Responsibility
Personal life	Advancement
Relationship with subordinates	Growth
Status	
Security	

Source: F. Herzberg, 'One more time: how do you motivate employees?' *Harvard Business Review*, January–February 1968.

unhygienic one can lead to trouble. In contrast are the *satisfiers* that people will work for and want more of. These tend to be intrinsic to the person. For example, having responsibility often makes people want more responsibility. If the work itself is interesting, then people will want more of that kind of work. Herzberg did his work among middle-class, professional Americans. It may be that other groups do not react to the same satisfiers. However, his ideas have been very popular among managers; they seem to fit in with a lot of their experience.

Two theories that add important dimensions to the models of Maslow and Herzberg are those of K. Lewin and V. Vroom. Lewin's 'field theory' emphasizes that individuals operate in a field of forces that represent subjective perceptions about the environment, the importance of a goal and the psychological distance of that goal.[3] Lewin uses it to try to account for the difference of motivation in people at different times. For example, you and I might both want to meet Harrison Ford. I see the circumstances as far too difficult; the goal of seeing him is not compelling enough to overcome the psychological distance to make any effort to see him worth while. You, however, may be in more favourable circumstances, may want to see him enough to overcome the psychological distance between him and you.

Vroom's 'expectancy theory' proposes that motivation is a product of the value that individuals place on the possible results of their actions and the expectation that their goal will be achieved.[4] The importance of this approach is that it emphasizes the individuality and variability of motivation rather than the generalizations of Maslow and Herzberg.

Motivating people at work

Some managers feel that motivation at work is no longer an issue because automation and other technologies have replaced the most tedious jobs, where getting motivated staff was difficult. Consider, however, how we as customers now expect better standards than we used to from service industries, the public sector and other organizations. The implication for managers in those sectors is that staff still need to be motivated to work well. So motivation at work remains an issue for most managers.

Many managers have conservative beliefs about motivating people. Many believe in a 'carrot and stick' approach: colleagues and subordinates will only work for obvious extrinsic rewards or punishment for errors. Slightly more sophisticated managers believe that it is just a matter of 'finding the right button to press', then people will work enthusiastically and skilfully. I hope to have persuaded you by now that things are not as simple as either of these two models.

Steers and Porter give a more systematic brief summary of the patterns of managerial approaches to motivation (see figure 8).[5] All these approaches can be discerned in current employing organizations. All managerial approaches to motivation suggest that managing motivation is a conscious and intentional recognition of individual differences. It is managing the work environment or 'climate', with the expected outcome that work will be better done. 'Motivating people at work' means ensuring that they are willing to work, to a standard, for the rewards offered.

Figure 8
General patterns of managerial approaches to motivation

Traditional model	Human relations model	Human resources model
Assumptions	*Assumptions*	*Assumptions*
1. Work is inherently distasteful to most people	1. People want to feel useful and important	1. Work is not inherently distasteful. People want to contribute to meaningful goals which they have helped establish
2. What they do is less important than what they earn for doing it	2. People desire to belong and to be recognized as individuals	
3. Few want or can handle work which requires creativity, self-direction, or self-control	3. These needs are more important than money in motivating people to work	2. Most people can exercise far more creative, responsible self-direction and self-control than their present jobs demand
Policies	*Policies*	*Policies*
1. The manager's basic task is to supervise and control subordinates closely	1. The manager's basic task is to make each worker feel useful and important	1. The manager's basic task is to make use of 'untapped' human resources
2. He or she must break tasks down into simple, repetitive, easily learned operations	2. He or she should keep subordinates informed and listen to their objections to his or her plans	2. He or she must create an environment in which all members may contribute to the limits of their ability
3. He or she must establish detailed work routines and procedures, and enforce them firmly but fairly	3. The manager should allow subordinates to exercise some self-direction and self-control on routine matters	3. He or she must encourage full participation on important matters, continually broadening subordinate self-direction and control
Expectations	*Expectations*	*Expectations*
1. People can tolerate work if the pay is decent and the boss is fair	1. Sharing information with subordinates and involving them in routine decisions will satisfy their basic needs to belong and to feel important	1. Expanding subordinate influence, self-direction and self-control will lead to direct improvements in operating efficiency
2. If tasks are simple enough and people are closely controlled, they will produce up to standard	2. Satisfying these needs will improve morale and reduce resistance to formal authority— subordinates will 'willingly cooperate'	2. Work satisfaction may improve as a 'by-product' of subordinates making full use of their resources

Source: R. M. Steers and L. W. Porter (eds.), *Motivation and work behaviour*, fourth edition, London, McGraw-Hill, 1987.

Figure 9
Variables affecting the motivational process in
organizational settings

I. *Individual* *characteristics*	II. *Job characteristics* *(examples)*	III. *Work environment* *characteristics*
1. Interests	Types of intrinsic rewards	1. Immediate work environment
2. Attitudes (examples)	Degree of autonomy	• Peers • Supervisor(s)
• Towards self • Towards job • Towards aspects of the work situation	Amount of direct performance feedback	2. Organizational actions • Reward practices • System-wide rewards
3. Needs (examples)	Degree of variety in tasks	• Individual rewards • Organizational climate
• Security • Social • Achievement		

Source: R. M. Steers *and* L. W. Porter (eds.), *Motivation and work behaviour,* fourth edition, London, McGraw-Hill, 1987, p. 21.

What affects the motivational process?

Steers and Porter indicate (see figure 9) some of the more important variables which influence employee motivation.[6] Part I of this book deals with the variables you might find under 'Individual characteristics'. If you look back you will recall that we examined how each of us perceives the world differently, with different personalities. Because of our experiences we have different attitudes to work and are looking for different types of satisfaction from it. All these things will affect our motivation, what we are willing to do at work in return for the rewards offered or perceived as offered. A good manager will take these individual variations into account when organizing the work to be done, and not treat everyone the same.

I will deal with Steers and Porter's second two groups, job characteristics and work environment characteristics, in more detail in Part III of this book as they are more directly related to the managing of motivation of people.

What is not motivating: implications for managers

Steers and Porter's variables (figure 9) are a useful checklist for managers. Clearly you can do little about the first column, individual characteristics, except when recruiting (see chapter 9). But difficulties can arise in the second and third columns about which something can be done. Anything on the list can be done badly. Chapter 13 deals with what to do when some of these lead to poor performance.

Perhaps it is also worth emphasising the point (made in chapter 8) that those managers who have an *agenda* of things to do, and a suitable *network* of contacts to get them done, are likely to have greater credibility with their colleagues. This will help in getting willing, co-operative work, i.e. in motivating people. It is the colleague, or boss, who is seen as out of touch or not pulling their weight who has most trouble getting things done, or motivating people to work.

Summary statements for managers

* We are initially motivated by the primary needs of our being. Only when they are satisfied do the secondary needs become important.
* At work these secondary needs are most important; they are socially determined, learnt needs.
* Motivation is affected by individual, job and organizational characteristics.
* Motivating people at work means different things to different people.

References

1 A. H. MASLOW, *Motivation and personality*. New York, Harper & Row, 1954.
2 F. Herzberg, 'One more time: how do you motivate employees?' *Harvard Business Review*, January–February 1968.
3 K. LEWIN, *Field theory in social science*, ed. D. Cartwright. London, Tavistock Publications, 1952.
4 V. VROOM and E. DECI, *Management and motivation*. London, Penguin Books, 1974.

5　R. M. STEERS and L. W. PORTER (eds.), *Motivation and work behaviour,*
　fourth edition. London, McGraw-Hill, 1987, p. 16.
6　*Ibid.,* p. 21.

5

Individual Orientation to Work

We all have different reasons for going to work and we want different things from work. Some of us are looking for totally involving jobs that offer opportunities for responsibility and recognition, for example becoming general manager. Others are looking for a little more money and the freedom to get on with things away from work.

The last three chapters were based mainly on psychological models and findings. This one uses the models and findings of sociology to look at the interplay between the individual and the structures of working life. How is it that we have devised a vast range of ways of making a living? Why is it that the meaning of work is so different from one person to another? Can we explain why the work experience varies?

The importance of work

Western culture places heavy emphasis on gainful employment, 'work'. The problems of the newly retired or redundant are due to their being excluded from work. Many women speak of themselves as 'only a housewife', as if that were somehow less valuable than other forms of work. Going out to work is important beyond itself for such things as self-esteem, status, belonging, as well as for the money and the experience. The feelings expressed by the unemployed, newly retired or redundant arise not just because of reduced income but because they feel less valued by their peers and families. Why is this?

The work ethic has been a strong force in the development of modern societies. It derived from the Protestant ethic and defines work as having an intrinsic value to the person doing it. Originally a connection was made between conscientious labour, disciplined application and the hope of salvation. The hope of salvation may now have disappeared but there is still a strong cultural assumption that work is important for individual worth. Max Weber, one of the founding fathers of sociology, suggested that salvation may have been replaced by the appeal of material possessions.[1] But the work ethic continues, with the idea of duty at work still having some of the connotations of a religious edict.

The fundamental assumption that work is more than just a means of making enough money to live is seen in many theoretical models of how people are motivated, or how organizations are best set up. For example, the writings of Maslow and Herzberg, mentioned in the previous chapter, suggest that the fully mature person seeks work that gives autonomy, discretion and the opportunity for self-actualization. They make out that human nature is such that we need this sort of work to fulfil our potential and achieve contentment. Sociology adds the important *caveat* that it is socially defined: concepts such as 'self-actualization' are culturally determined, in this case by the developed Western world. It is not only management writers who argue that work is central to human activity. Marxist approaches also take the basic view that work is fundamental to human happiness. They argue that the problem of work is not having to do it, but that it is not always satisfying.

P. D. Anthony suggests that the ideology of work, whether expressed by management or by radical writers, is required only when some human groups require the labour of others to meet economic ends.[2] Anthony questions our cultural attachment to work. Such questioning has become more important since he wrote, owing to the rise in unemployment and the advent of post-industrial society. Have we reached a stage where not everyone can be in paid employment? Even though a demographic shortage of school leavers is expected in the 1990s, everyone is competing for the well qualified, not for the unskilled. Are we condemning some members of society to a second-class existence? Or are there other activities that can be made central to our lives, with work taking a secondary, or instrumental, role, aiming merely to make a living?

Handy, as ever, has interesting things to say about this. He suggests in his book *The Future of Work* that the family may become increasingly a focus for many.[3] Handy also predicts that many of us will have a portfolio of work: we shall individually contract to do particular things and collect a 'portfolio' of different contracts with different employers. This has already been seen in the rise of peripheral, as opposed to core, workers in many types of employment. The core workers are full-time, permanent employees, central to the business, who are well looked after. Peripheral workers are those on a part-time, temporary or contract basis. Such portfolio work suits many people who want to control their own time and achieve a balance between work and other pursuits.

Orientation to work

What is the meaning of work for individuals? Does work have the same importance for us all? Clearly not. Is there some inevitable connection between certain work conditions and experiences and particular attitudes and feelings? What do we mean by job satisfaction? Is it the same for us all?

Most studies in this field have been done on manual labour in manufacturing workplaces. This is partly because this group of people are easy to study, as they have less to hide, and partly because they have been seen as a problem by management. However, it is clear that the technology used by workers will constrain the way in which the work can be organized, which in turn will influence the attitude and behaviour of the workers. For example, some technologies, like printing, allow social groupings at work. Others, such as car assembly, do not.

The classic study which introduced the concept of orientation to work was that of Goldthorpe *et al.*, who examined the attitude and behaviour of assembly line workers at the Vauxhall plant in Luton. One important conclusion emerged:

> The question of satisfaction from work cannot in the end be usefully considered except in relation to the more basic question of what we would term orientation to work. Until one knows something of the way in which workers order their wants and expectations relative to their employment— until one knows what *meaning* work has for them—one is not in a position to understand what overall assessment of their job satisfaction may most appropriately be made in their case.[4]

They went on to discuss various orientations to work. They particularly concentrated on what is termed an 'instrumental' orientation to work, by which they meant:

The primary meaning of work is as a means to an end, or ends, external to the work situation; that is work is regarded as a means of acquiring the income necessary to support a valued way of life of which work itself is not an integral part. Work is therefore experienced as mere 'labour' in the sense of an expenditure of effort which is made for extrinsic rather than intrinsic rewards.[5]

An instrumental orientation means that employees will put up with unpleasant work as long as, in their view, the financial reward is satisfactory.

Goldthorpe *et al.* also identified two other orientations to work, the bureaucratic and the solidaristic. The bureaucratic orientation describes those people who sought to give service to a company over a long time in return for a career that saw some promotion and increased status, security and pay. The solidaristic orientation characterized those people who, in addition to an economic orientation, also valued group loyalty to their mates.

Another approach to this area is that of the psychologist E. H. Schein.[6] He argues that for everyone there is some aspect of their attachment to work that they will not abandon. He calls these aspects 'career anchors'. They act as the dominant guiding force in our working life. Examples are:

- Autonomy.
- Creativity.
- Organizational security.
- Managerial competence.
- Technical competence.

Schein argues that each of us will tolerate reorganization and change at work but will not compromise on our career anchor. For example, a manager who values autonomy will move companies rather than be constrained by regulations. In contrast, a manager who values organizational security will tolerate all sorts of changes rather than look elsewhere for employment.

An instrumental orientation is about extrinsic (i.e. outside the person) rewards from work. It contrasts with the assumption underlying the models of Maslow and Herzberg that intrinsic (i.e. within the person) rewards from work are the ultimate goal of everyone. Not all workers feel that they are looking for self-actualization through work.

Research in this area is problematic. Discussing the meaning of work involves our basic assumptions about morals, power, equality, the rights of individuals, and so on, all of which are political. The same findings can be differently interpreted. Another problem is, what exactly do we mean by job satisfaction and the meaning of work? Is it always the same thing? As Fox says:

> . . . men can at one and the same time (i) expect work to be largely instrumental in nature (ii) become satisfied with (i.e. resigned to) this situation, and, (iii) wish that it could be otherwise—that intrinsic rewards were also open to them.[7]

Alienation

This concept, used in sociology and elsewhere, was originally formulated by Marx to analyse the effect of capitalism on people. Marx referred to people's detachment, estrangement and loss of control over their lives in capitalist society.[8] Alienation is about the separation of people. It is applied to the way we feel cut off from important decisions, people or outcomes. The work we do can feel alien and oppressive. It is thought that it is the way work is organized that leads to this alienation, rather than particular work processes.

Individuals can be alienated from *other people* because the relationships have become calculating, self-interested and untrusting. The phenomenon of yuppies in the 1980s provided an example of the sort of people who have become alienated from others and are able to behave callously towards them without a sense of embarrassment.

People can be alienated from the *product* of their labour, when the end product is not seen or is remote from their control. It can also happen when people are not involved in the original decisions about what the work is to be. The classic example is large-scale manufacturing, as in car plants,[9] compared with traditional crafts such as pottery where the worker sees the results of their labour.

People are alienated from *their own labour* when they are unable to get the satisfactions of work because they are controlled by others and so are meeting someone else's requirements and standards, not their own. Marx argues that alienation is an objective state. We may not feel dissatisfied with our job but we may be missing out on something much more rewarding. An example can be seen in those managers who have been made redundant and have developed alternative activities which they find more worthwhile than their former employment. Before redundancy they were alienated.

R. Blauner studied factory workers and their feelings about their work.[10] He argues that alienation consists of four conditions or states: powerlessness, meaninglessness, isolation and self-estrangement. Powerlessness is felt when people are controlled. Meaninglessness is felt where they do not understand the co-ordination or purpose of their bit of the work. Isolation is felt when they do not feel they belong. Self-estrangement is felt where they are detached from their work: there is no sense of involvement, it is only a means to an end. This view of alienation can be applied to any large, formal work organization, not just those in capitalist societies.

If someone is alienated at work their orientation to the job is likely to be instrumental, with less emphasis on intrinsic rewards than in the case of more committed colleagues. Examples of both alienated and non-alienated workers can be found at all levels in any hierarchy. Many a reorganization, or take-over, has left senior managers feeling alienated from the new organization in all of Blauner's ways.

Vocational choice

In the considerable literature on the processes leading to people's starting work the emphasis is either on the individual's choice of occupation or on the determining effect of external factors. The first would underline the psychological development of self-concept. This develops as abilities, aptitudes and interests grow. Much career guidance is based on this material. It may well be that you can recall being given questionnaires in the fourth year of secondary school, so that you could explore your interests and start the process of vocational choice.

The second sort of literature places the emphasis on the roles we play at home, at school and in our first employment. These roles provide the settings in which the individual is socialized and learns to select appropriate work roles. For example, many young girls are socialized into the role of caring and nurturing others.

Figure 10
Factors affecting career choice

Non-work structural factors	Individual approaching work	Work sphere structural factors
Class Family Education Race Gender Media and peer influences	Resources of cash, skills, knowledge, physique Motives, expectations, interests and aspirations	Occupational structure and prevailing labour market (number and type of job vacancies)

Source: T. Watson, *Sociology, work and industry*, London, Routledge, 1980, p. 127.

This makes the work role of nursing and looking after children attractive to many teenage girls.

A third strand is the structural limitation on the choices open to us. For many it is a case of fitting into whatever jobs are available. The well qualified middle-class white female in Croydon has more choices than the unqualified working-class black male in Liverpool. The career of any individual is very much influenced by the combination of class, family and education. The occupation of the parents will be very influential in deciding on a career. This will be directly because they encourage, or discourage, their children to follow in their footsteps. Also indirectly as the parent encourages the child to pursue something they themselves would have liked to have done.

Watson suggests a simple model to bring these processes together (see figure 10).[11] We all have a different combination of class, family, education, race, gender and influences from our peers and the media. These will influence our career choice. They will also affect how each of us approaches work in terms of the resources available to us – for example, the money, skills and knowledge we have. We are all different, too, in our physique, motives, expectations, interests and aspirations, which will affect how we approach work. These in turn will be affected by aspects of work such as how it is organized, what types of jobs there are, and whether there are plenty of vacancies or not. This simple model summarizes how the influence of background, individual capacities and opportunities available affects the career choice. These factors come together to give each of us an orientation towards particular types of work. Values, wants and preferences are checked against available jobs to see which match best. The employee will weigh up the costs of mental and physical labour, loss of freedom and fatigue against the benefits of money, job satisfaction, social rewards, power, status, and so on. The balance of preferences will be different for each of us. This leads to an implicit contract between the employer and the employee. Enid Mumford suggests that the degree of fit between the individual's needs and those of the organization will determine the employer's satisfaction with the employee and the employee's job satisfaction. She suggests there are five contractual areas: psychological, efficiency, ethical, knowledge and task structure.[12] (See chapter 13.)

Individual careers

The previous section looked at some of the factors affecting an individual's initial choice of work. What happens after this? Are there typical patterns in different occupational groups? How do we continue to make choices in the work we do?

One of the ways people achieve a sense of coherence in their working lives is by adopting the idea of a career. It may be an occupational career or an organizational career. The career is the sequence of positions that are typically associated with an occupation or organization. Different positions usually mean different levels of prestige, reward and influence. Movement can be upward, downward or sideways. Professional and bureaucratic careers tend to be like a ladder leading upwards. Sports careers tend to be short, with a peak in the middle. Acting careers are typically insecure. Many manual careers change very little over the years. Describing the typical career patterns of various occupations can help people make suitable career choices. For example, there have been several studies of managers' careers.[13]

Alban-Metcalfe and Nicholson conclude a study of the career development of British managers[14] with the following five points:

- Managers are concerned more about the nature of their job than its material rewards and setting.
- They are mobile.
- Job changes are even more rapid than people think because of internal changes within organizations.
- They have to adjust constantly to change.
- Job changes come about because of informal sources of information, so politics are important for promotion.

Many managers are encouraged to engage in some sort of career planning. Personnel departments have aided the process by claiming to have management development plans for individuals. On many courses individual managers are asked to fill in life plans that include some sort of career planning. One example is by Pedler *et al.*, who ask questions such as 'What are your goals for your future job or career?' and then ask you to consider how you might go about achieving them.[15] This emphasis on personal responsibility and autonomy in deciding careers is very popular, although most large organizations still have a 'fast track' for a few managers who are given a variety of experience to ensure they are groomed for senior posts later on.

Implications for managers

Much discussion about work motivation centres on whether people go to work just for the money, for the company of others, for extrinsic rewards, or because they want jobs that are inherently satisfying. The evidence from the Luton studies suggest that there are people willing to work for both reasons. As Mills wrote:

> Work may be a mere source of livelihood, or the most significant part of one's inner life; it may be experienced as expiation, or as an exuberant expression of self; as a bounden duty, or as a development of man's universal nature. Neither love nor hatred of work is inherent in man, or inherent in any given line of work.[16]

This suggests that managers need to understand that those who work with them may not have the same orientation to work as they have themselves. For example, many head teachers and deputy head teachers are horrified to find that some of their junior colleagues do not want to be involved in all the decisions within the school but look on teaching as confined only to working with the pupils. The mere fact that someone has a different orientation to work does not mean they will not do a good day's work. The concept of alienation alerts managers to some of the political and moral implications of their work. To what extent is it legitimate and appropriate to organize other people's work so that they are powerless, isolated, self-estranged or find work meaningless, in Blauner's phrases? Is it possible to reorganize the work so as to minimize these aspects of the experience? The authority and power of managers rest on moral foundations. Anthony argues that managers are abdicating responsibility if they do not control labour.[17] In Western industrialized societies the control usually needs to be considered legitimate by those subject to it.

The idea of some sort of implicit contract between employees and employers is useful for managers. What are the relative obligations in Mumford's five areas? A useful series of questions may be asked. Are the particular person and job adequately matched psychologically? For knowledge? In efficiency? Ethically? In the way the task is structured? This contract also has implications for the career of any one individual. Does the career promise the sunlit uplands of management by the time they are forty? Or is the career pattern very stable, with little change? How does it fit the individual's view of their own career?

Summary statements for managers

- Many people assume that work has greater importance than just earning enough to live on.
- Different people derive different satisfactions from work. Some look for extrinsic satisfactions, such as high pay. Others look for intrinsic satisfactions, such as interesting work.
- People, including managers, can be alienated from their work. They feel powerless, isolated; the work seems meaningless.
- Our career choices are influenced by our background, our resources and the openings available.

References

1 M. WEBER, *The Protestant ethic and the spirit of capitalism*. London, Allen & Unwin, 1965.
2 P. D. ANTHONY, *The ideology of work*. London, Tavistock Publications, 1977.
3 C. HANDY, *The future of work: a guide to changing society*. Oxford, Blackwell, 1984.
4 J. H. GOLDTHORPE, D. LOCKWOOD, F. BECHHOFER and J. PLATT, *The affluent worker in the class struggle*. Cambridge, Cambridge University Press, 1969, p, 36.
5 *Ibid.*, p. 39.
6 E. H. SCHEIN, *Organizational psychology*, third edition. Englewood Cliffs, N. J., Prentice Hall, 1980.
7 A. FOX, *A sociology of work in industry*. London, Collier Macmillan, 1971.
8 K. MARX, 'On alienation', in T. B. Bottomore and M. Rubel (eds.) *Karl Marx: selected writings in sociology and social philosophy*. Harmondsworth, Penguin Books, 1963.
9 See H. BEYNON, *Working for Ford*. Harmondsworth, Penguin Books, 1973.
10 R. BLAUNER, *Alienation and freedom: the factory worker and his industry*. Chicago, University of Chicago Press, 1967.
11 T. WATSON, *Sociology, work and industry*. London, Routledge, 1980, p. 127.
12 E. MUMFORD, 'Job satisfaction: a method of analysis, *Personnel Review*, summer 1972.
13 See, for example, R. MANSFIELD, M. POOLE, P. BLYTON and P. FROST, *The British manager in profile*, BIM Survey No. 51. London, British Institute of Management, 1981.
14 B. ALBAN-METCALFE and N. NICHOLSON, *The career development of British managers*. London, British Institute of Management, 1984.
15 M. PEDLER, J. BURGOYNE and T. BOYDELL, *A manager's guide to self-development*, second edition. Maidenhead, McGraw-Hill, 1986.
16 C. W. MILLS, *White collar: the American middle classes*. New York, Oxford University Press, 1956.
17 P. D. ANTHONY, *The foundation of management*. Tavistock Publications, London, 1986.

PART II
Working in Groups

6

Groups and Group Dynamics

Working in an organization inevitably means working in groups. To distinguish our activity at work from that of a mob we have to do various things such as make decisions, delegate authority and set boundaries between us and the rest of the world.[1] All these demands require us to get together in groups. A hospital could not care for patients, a restaurant serve meals nor a plastics company make containers without individuals coming together in groups of different sizes and types. The groups may be our immediate colleagues in a section or department. They can also be designed to fulfil a co-ordinating role, such as area or management groups. We also participate in temporary or part-time groups, such as meetings, working parties or task groups. It is hard to imagine any activity that does not involve some group work. The long-distance lorry driver, often taken as the epitome of the lone worker, has to co-operate with others to get the vehicle loaded and unloaded, with the correct paperwork and instructions.

Having conceded that groups are an inevitable part of work, how can we understand them and the way they work? Is there anything we can do to improve the way we work in groups?

Group theory and its application to work

Research on groups has taken various forms. Some of it was done years ago but, having achieved classic status in the literature of both social science and management, is included here. Such studies look at things like the effects of groups on decision-making, group stability and the different roles people play. If we look at the classic studies in turn we can see some pointers, warnings or confirmation of common sense that can be of help.

Some people have studied real groups working. For example, I.L. Janis studied the decision-making of United States foreign policy groups.[2] He found that a cohesive group of individuals,

sharing a common fate, exerts a strong pressure toward conformity. He found that President Kennedy's Bay of Pigs fiasco in Cuba and the disaster in Vietnam could not be accounted for by individual incompetence. He coined the phrase 'groupthink' to cover the exaggeration of irrational tendencies that seems to occur in groups. He argues that the group setting can magnify weakness of judgement.

Janis's 'groupthink' concept is perhaps most helpful as a warning that groups are not always a good thing. For example, when change is being proposed there is a tendency to dismiss those who are reluctant to support the innovations as dull, unimaginative, obstinate, behind the times—not one of us. It might just be that the proposed change is not so good after all, and the rest of us are suffering from some sort of groupthink. Another example is daring to question the received wisdom that groups of executives should always operate as teams. If groupthink can happen in senior policy groups we need to consider when groups are necessary and when they are not. David Casey points out that not all management groups need to be a team, and it can be a waste of time trying to create one if it is not necessary.[3]

Another study of real workings groups was undertaken by A. K. Rice in an Indian textile mill.[4] He concluded that the most productive group, and the most satisfactory to its members, was the pair, or a group with between six and twelve members. Group *stability* was most easily maintained where every member of the group could understand the others' skills and when there were only a few differences in status and prestige among them. It was beneficial for a group if disaffected members could move elsewhere.

Rice's study of the stability of groups gives us some strategies for building up long-lasting groups. For example, in departments where people need to work closely with each other and exchange ideas it seems that structures which do not emphasize differences of prestige or status are most likely to succeed. In secondary schools the most influential grouping is the department, such as science or humanities; it is there that the main decisions about what happens to the pupils take place. It is also with the department that most teachers identify. Most secondary school departments number between six and eight people, with few differences in status, and the teachers in a department are all concerned with the same subject. This all fits Rice's conclusions.

Others have studied groups of people in the rather artificial setting of the laboratory. For example, H.J. Leavitt examined which types of communication pattern were most appropriate for different tasks.[5] For the purposes of the experiment small groups of people were asked to communicate in different ways, as summarized in figure 11. The patterns illustrated by Leavitt represent typical situations at work. The wheel is like a regional sales team with four salespeople reporting to a regional manager. The chain is like a department, with two executives, B and D, each reporting to manager C and having assistants A and E. The Y is similar to an orthodox chain of command, with one person, B, who is outside and who communicates only with C, as in the case of a key supplier or customer. The circle and the completed network are like discussion groups, the circle being the unusual form most frequently found in experiments or training devices.

In an influential study R.F. Bales found that effective groups needed people who helped get things done, that is, they were concerned with the 'what' or task facing the group.[6] They also needed people who were concerned with the 'how', or social and emotional side of working in a group. Team members who were task-oriented were the most influential; those who were interested in the positive social emotional aspects were the most liked. He developed a series of observable categories from this study that are summarized in figure 12.

People whose behaviour falls within areas A, B and C can all help to make the group work better, whereas those demonstrating behaviour in area D can be destructive. Next time you are in a group—for example, at a meeting—take a sheet with these twelve types of behaviour listed down the side. Put the initials of the participants across the top and then tick the respective box for each type of behaviour, both verbal and non-verbal, that you observe. You may be surprised to find who is really most helpful to the group in getting things done or maintaining cohesion; it is not always the noisiest. Do not forget the non-verbals such as a smile, a nod of the head, pushing back from the table. The labels *a, b, c, d, e* and *f* refer to the different processes that groups have to deal with, which are discussed later in this chapter.

The work of Bales has been particularly useful as a training device in concentrating people's attention on the 'how' of group working. Where meetings end in frustration or groups feel irritated with each other it is usually here that the problem lies. No amount

Figure 11
Types of communication networks in groups

The pattern of communication in groups can have important conse-quences for efficiency and member satisfaction. The patterns can vary in the number of potential channels available, the equality of the communication possible and how centralized the pattern is. Different patterns are effective for different tasks. Some common patterns, based on the research of Leavitt, are shown here.

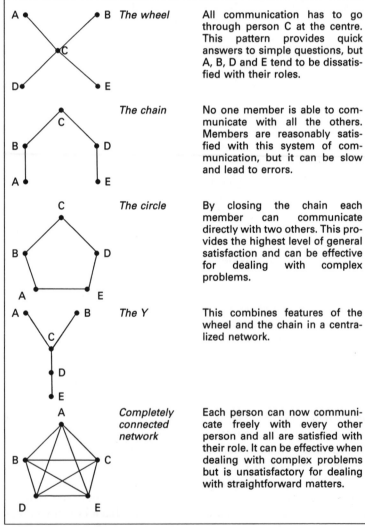

The wheel	All communication has to go through person C at the centre. This pattern provides quick answers to simple questions, but A, B, D and E tend to be dissatis-fied with their roles.
The chain	No one member is able to com-municate with all the others. Members are reasonably satis-fied with this system of com-munication, but it can be slow and lead to errors.
The circle	By closing the chain each member can communicate directly with two others. This pro-vides the highest level of general satisfaction and can be effective for dealing with complex problems.
The Y	This combines features of the wheel and the chain in a centra-lized network.
Completely connected network	Each person can now communi-cate freely with every other person and all are satisfied with their role. It can be effective when dealing with complex problems but is unsatisfactory for dealing with straightforward matters.

Source: Based on H. J. Leavitt, 'Some aspects of certain communication patterns on group performance,' *Journal of Abnormal and Social Psychology*, 45, 1951, pp. 38–50.

Figure 12
Bales' interaction process categories

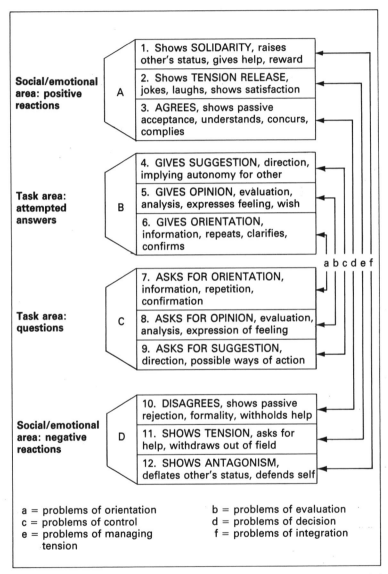

Social/emotional area: positive reactions

A
1. Shows SOLIDARITY, raises other's status, gives help, reward
2. Shows TENSION RELEASE, jokes, laughs, shows satisfaction
3. AGREES, shows passive acceptance, understands, concurs, complies

Task area: attempted answers

B
4. GIVES SUGGESTION, direction, implying autonomy for other
5. GIVES OPINION, evaluation, analysis, expresses feeling, wish
6. GIVES ORIENTATION, information, repeats, clarifies, confirms

Task area: questions

C
7. ASKS FOR ORIENTATION, information, repetition, confirmation
8. ASKS FOR OPINION, evaluation, analysis, expression of feeling
9. ASKS FOR SUGGESTION, direction, possible ways of action

Social/emotional area: negative reactions

D
10. DISAGREES, shows passive rejection, formality, withholds help
11. SHOWS TENSION, asks for help, withdraws out of field
12. SHOWS ANTAGONISM, deflates other's status, defends self

a b c d e f

a = problems of orientation
c = problems of control
e = problems of managing tension

b = problems of evaluation
d = problems of decision
f = problems of integration

Source: Based on R. F. Bales, *Interaction process analysis*, Reading, Mass., Addison-Wesley, 1950.

of trying to specify the objectives more carefully or putting things in writing will make the group work better. What is needed is some attention to the social/emotional side of things. Equally, groups that have a great time, laughing and joking, ultimately frustrate their object as work groups if nothing gets done. John Kotter's description of the work of general managers as being composed of agendas of things that need doing and networks of contacts to get them done[7] is very much the same sort of idea (see chapter 8). The important point is that both 'what' and 'how' are necessary. Groups that concentrate only on the task in hand will be as ineffective as those that concentrate only on getting on with one another.

R.M. Belbin developed the work of Bales and looked at the different roles that are necessary for management teams.[8] He identified eight:

- The *company worker*, who works to keep the organization's interests to the fore.
- The *chair*, who ensures that all views are heard and keeps things moving.
- The *shaper*, who influences by argument and by following particular topics.
- The *ideas person*, or *plant*, who contributes novel suggestions.
- The *resource investigator*, who evaluates whether contributions are practical and finds out where and how to obtain resources.
- The *monitor/evaluator*, who assesses how valid the contributions are and the extent to which the team is meeting its objectives.
- The *team worker*, who maintains the group by joking and agreeing.
- The *completer/finisher*, who tries to get things done and suggests conclusions.

At different times each of these roles has to be filled if a team is to work effectively. Most of us fill more than one of these roles but a consistent pattern emerges. Several management training devices are based on these roles.

Belbin and his roles have given rise to many an amusing hour on management courses when colleagues agree or disagree with the labelling arrived at after filling in a questionnaire. Perhaps the most useful practical outcome is the realization that work groups need a variety of personalities if they are to function well. The inevitable cloning, and the problems it creates, which can occur where selection is based only on the principle of 'Do I like this person and can I work with them?' might be avoided if it is recalled that differences can make work more effective. The art, of course, is in getting the right differences.

Sources of group cohesion and team-building

B.W. Tuckman suggests there are various stages small groups go through before they become mature enough in their relations to be able to work together consistently.[9] These stages are set out in figure 13. Tuckman's stages are helpful in showing that group development takes time to become effective. The time it takes will vary according to how long the group is going to work together. For a team that is to be together a long time it may take many months, because the degree of commitment required from each member is so high and the risk of personal failure so great. If the team is convening as a short-term, part-time group, e.g. to arrange the office party, then the individual risk is less and tolerance is higher. Individual tolerance of the process will vary; there is always someone who will make a comment like 'If we don't get something done soon, we shall be here all night.'

A number of theorists, as well as Tuckman, have suggested that a group develops through a fairly predictable sequence of phases. Each phase has at its core a particular issue which the group must at least partially resolve before going on to the next phase. W. C. Schutz, and E. H. Schein both suggest that the concern of early meetings is invariably the issue of *inclusion*—to what extent do I feel part of this group?[10] It follows that individuals are most concerned about themselves at the beginning. There are likely to be rapid changes of topic as everyone raises issues that concern them, and conflict is highly probable. Time needs to be taken to allow everyone the opportunity to express themselves and to establish an identity within the group. It is only then that the group is ready to work.

Bales and Belbin tell us something about how teams keep together. Others have studied the *group norms* that are developed through this process: the expectations, or implicit rules, that groups develop to define what is acceptable behaviour and what is not. To realize how common these norms are, think of the difficulty of

Figure 13
Stages in the growth of group cohesion and performance

Stage of development	Process	Outcome
1. Forming	There is anxiety, dependence on leader; testing to find out the nature of the situation and what behaviour is acceptable	Members find out what the task is, what the rules are and what methods are appropriate
2. Storming	Conflict between sub-groups, rebellion against leader; opinions are polarized; resistance 'to control by group	Emotional resistance to demands of task
3. Norming	Development of group cohesion; norms emerge; resistance is overcome and conflicts are patched up; mutual support and sense of group identity	Open exchange of views and feelings; co-operation develops
4. Performing	Interpersonal problems are resolved; interpersonal structure becomes the means of getting things done; roles are flexible and functional	Solutions to problems emerge; there are constructive attempts to complete tasks and energy is now available for effective work

Source: Based on B. W. Tuckman, 'Development sequences in small groups', *Psychological Bulletin*, 63, 1965, pp. 384–99.

being the only new member of a work group, particularly if one is supposed to be an 'experienced' worker. Newcomers are expected to comply with the group norms until they have gone through the socializing process of learning the expected behaviour. Eventually the norms become their own, and are internalized, or they are rejected and the newcomer remains outside the group. These group norms serve several purposes. Cartwright and Zander[11] list the main ones as:

Task. Norms develop that influence the way in which the group will achieve its goals. What is considered a fair day's work for a fair day's pay varies considerably from one group to another. What are the norms for your own group, and who has helped establish them? Did you inherit a set when you took up your present post?

Maintenance. Norms develop within the group that help to keep it together, for instance styles of speaking, little games that are played on each other, or cliquey behaviour. What special behaviour distinguishes your work group from your colleagues in other groups? Do you, for instance, have little rituals associated with coffee or Fridays? What nicknames do you have at work?

Defining relations with others. Certain norms define how members should treat significant people, for example the boss, or other groups within the same organization. What is the normal way for you to speak to the boss at work? How did you get the boss to treat you in a way that fits the group norms? Are there some parts of the organization your group does not consult? One group I know does not consult the computing department when it has a computing problem. The computer people in their purpose-built office are seen as too ivory-tower. 'Real people don't work in glass houses.'

Effective and ineffective decision-making groups

So far we have concentrated on the *process* side of group work. That is the way people work together. It is also important to look at the *content*—what the group has to do. Here are a series of questions to ask when setting up a working party, a task force or some other temporary group. See also figure 16 on pages 90–91.

If the group is charged with making decisions there are several issues that need clearing first. What are the terms of reference for the decision-making? Can the group really make a decision, or can it only make a recommendation? What decisions are allowed: are there some that are not? Have any decisions already been made about this matter that cannot be changed? Are there some conclusions that would be unacceptable?

Consideration also needs to be given to who should be in the group that is to make the decision. On the one hand all those involved in a decision are committed to making it work; those who were not involved can find all sorts of reasons why it will not work. On the other, if too many folk are included the dynamics of the group become impossible to handle, as many people do not like speaking in front of large groups. So who should attend? All those with the slightest interest? A variety of personalities, to ensure a lively discussion? Only those with expertise in this area? Do some people have a right to get involved?

Once the terms of reference and membership have been decided the group can get started. The various phases will need to be gone through, but some systematic consideration of such things as types of contributions, agenda and style of minutes will help the decision-making as well.

Ineffective decision-making may be due to a lack of task orientation or a lack of cohesion among the group. The person responsible, for example the chair of a meeting, can try to do something about this. It is important to focus discussion on disagreements that need resolving. Asking for clarification where other members have obviously not understood a speaker, or look puzzled, can also keep the discussion focused. Ensuring beforehand that there is a suitable balance of views, styles and authority will help to hold the group together. Finally the group leader should seek workable hypotheses from the discussion and put them to the group for acceptance whenever possible. The important thing in effective group decision-making is to look after both the content and the process.

Co-operation and competitiveness between groups

In most working environments the different working groups have to be co-ordinated in some formal way. The various guides to organizational structure such as organization charts and job descriptions are used to ensure that the work of each person and each group is sufficiently differentiated from and suitably co-ordinated with others to make the whole work together. Methods of doing this vary, depending on the predictability and nature of the job. In a restaurant where the nature of the job is fairly predictable the relationship between the people working in the kitchen and those working in the dining room is often very formal, based on written orders, with little social chit-chat. By contrast social workers who have unpredictable problems to deal with often have quite informal contacts with each other across groups as they find they need to use each other's expertise and resources. For those who hold a 'unitary' view of organizations (see chapter 1) the idea of groups competing within the same company is unattractive. They try to avoid it by harmonization of methods, procedures and objectives. They attach great importance to team work and corporate identity. For those who hold a 'pluralist' view (again, see chapter 1), competition between groups is regarded as normal and to be encouraged, as it will bring out the best in people. For people holding this belief, allowing groups some autonomy, even if this entails a measure of duplication, ensures that everyone is close to the customer and maximizes their contribution. In their influential book *In Search of Excellence* Peters and Waterman[12] quote examples of first-rate companies allowing different groups, which might be seen as competing for ideas and resources to coexist. Peters and Waterman felt that it contributed to success.

One development in recent times that requires co-ordination has been the distinction between core and periphery workers. As we saw in chapter 5, core workers are those the organization depends on to conduct its business. They will be full-time, permanently employed, well looked after and trained. Periphery workers are all those on temporary, part-time or contract arrangements. The organization employs them for specific work and does not involve them in long-term plans or commitments. Managing these two different groups or a mixture of them can be a problem. The peripheral staff will need far more detailed specification of what they are to do, whilst the core staff may well be involved in deciding what is to be done. The core staff are more committed to the organization, which raises various questions. For example, should part-time staff be involved in team briefing sessions? What about the contract staff? Who do you invite to the Christmas party?

The more complex the organization the more groups there will be. They will need co-ordination. A useful concept here is 'loose—tight' to describe the amount of autonomy and control allowed to the various groups. (See chapter 8.) K. Weick says, '. . . it is easy to overmanage an organisation . . . it is an excess rather than deficiency of intervention that lies at the heart of many organisational problems.'[13]

Implications for managers

Working is often about working in groups. Some are long-term groups such as one's colleagues. Others are short-term groups of semi-strangers, such as decision groups, project teams or co-ordinating groups. Any one of us will play different roles in different groups at different stages of their development. By understanding some of the underlying processes outlined in this chapter we are more likely to make an effective contribution to the groups we belong to and to be able to help others do so as well.

The effective managers are the ones who can work in a variety of groups. They understand the dynamics and are able to influence events towards a desired outcome. They understand that this is not always achieved by making statements so much as by nursing others towards making their own contribution and so getting the commitment to making the outcome work.

Summary statements for managers

* Research gives us clear directives about 'groupthink', group stability, patterns of communication and the balance of team members.
* Groups develop through various stages before they can work well. They maintain cohesion through group norms.
* Effective groups look after the content, the 'what', and the process, the 'how', of their meetings.
* How the various groups of an organization are co-ordinated will be determined by the nature of the organization.

References

1 C. ARGYRIS and D. SCHÖN, *Organizational learning*. Reading, Mass., Addison-Wesley, 1978.
2 I. L. JANIS, *Victims of groupthink*. Boston, Mass., Houghton Mifflin, 1972.

3   D. CASEY, 'When is a team not a team?' *Personnel Management*, January 1985, pp. 26–9.

4   A. K. RICE, *Productivity and social organisation*. London, Tavistock Publications, 1958.

5   H. J. LEAVITT, 'Some aspects of certain communication patterns on group performance'. *Journal of Abnormal and Social Psychology*, 45, 1951, pp. 38–50.

6   R. F. BALES, *Interaction process analysis*. Reading, Mass., Addison-Wesley, 1950.

7   J. KOTTER, *The general managers*. New York, Free Press, 1982.

8   R. M. BELBIN, *Management teams: why they succeed or fail*. London, Heinemann, 1981.

9   B. W. TUCKMAN, 'Development sequences in small groups'. *Psychological Bulletin*, 63, 1965, pp. 384–99.

10 W. C. SCHUTZ, *The interpersonal world*. New York, Science and Behavior Books, 1966; E. H. SCHEIN, *Process consultation: its role in organization development*. Reading, Mass., Addison-Wesley, 1969.

11 D. CARTWRIGHT and A. ZANDER, *Group dynamics*, third edition. London, Tavistock Publications, 1968.

12 T. J. PETERS and R. H. WATERMAN, *In search of excellence*. London, Harper & Row, 1982.

13 K. WEICK, *The social psychology of organizing*. Reading, Mass., Addison-Wesley, 1979, p. 60.

7

Communication

Consider these typical snatches of everyday conversation at work.
'Nobody ever tells me anything!'
'The customers always seem to know before us.'
'Oh, no! Not more bumph in my in-tray!'
'I'm sorry ... I didn't know about it.'
'Well, you really should have. It was in your in-tray last week.'
These remarks demonstrate the problems of communication in any large organization. Variations of them were in fact all heard in secondary schools. On a human relations basis it seems impossible to satisfy everyone all the time, and on an efficiency basis it seems equally impossible to get the message through every time. This can be very frustrating and bewildering to those few individuals who can justifiably pride themselves on their efficiency in this respect. No matter how well the system of communication looks on paper, there will always be occasions when it breaks down. We should not be too surprised by this. We are, after all, only human! There are, however, usually some ways of improving our own and an organization's communication, even if perfection is impossible.

Poor communication is very often blamed for all organizational ills. Consultants are often brought in to look at communication in the organization: this, it is assumed, will solve the problem. Usually communication problems are just a presenting symptom, and the problem, like the solution, is elsewhere. It may lie in all sorts of other things, such as the organization structure, management hierarchies, status distinction, lack of trust, lack of clarity about what staff are trying to do, problems of power distribution, lack of credibility on the part of senior staff or lack of consensus on objectives. Communication is all things to all people, and everyone will have their own ideas about what they expect to find in this chapter. Not all of it will be here. You may find other chapters in the book, or others in the series, more helpful in analysing what initially feels like a communication problem but in reality is an organizational, structural or personal problem.

It is also important to remember the pluralist–unitarist distinction discussed earlier. Perceptions, orientations and expectations about communications are likely to be different at shop-floor or office level than at the top of the organization. Pluralists, such as those with an employee relations perspective, would argue for a variety of approaches as appropriate. However the Human Resource Management approach – unitarist – is to emphasize individuals working together and ensuring everyone receives similar communications. Both models can be found at work in organizations. It is simply a matter of belief and fundamental approach to the politics of organizations which type of communication a particular manager is likely to use.

The purpose of communication at work is not only to keep people informed. It is also the main means of influencing each other's behaviour. It is therefore an important part of management skills as we try to influence each other towards agreed actions.

Communication in the organization

One of the effects of organizational life is a tendency to feel distanced from the centre of actions that affect our lives. The irony is that this distancing has often been exacerbated by noble attempts to compensate for it with more committees, handbooks, procedures and representatives. Often an increase in the information available only decreases the amount of communication! The reason is that information can become communication only when the process is two-way.

In organizations, as elsewhere, most of the communication that takes place is interpersonal, that is, face-to-face. But some communication strategies are deliberately established, usually by managers, to enable particular sorts of communication to take place. The process is sometimes called *organizational communication*, although obviously an organization does not communicate; only the people working in it can do that.

H.W. Greenbaum has developed a model for auditing communication in an organization.[1] He suggests four main objectives that managers have for organizational communication:

- *Regulation:* seeking to ensure that employee behaviour conforms with organizational objectives, e.g. a departmental meeting about quality.
- *Innovation:* seeking to change aspects of organizational functioning in specific directions, e.g. how to reduce waste.
- *Integration:* maintaining the morale of the work force and developing a feeling of identity with the organization and its members, e.g. staff socials.
- *Information:* giving the mainly factual information that people need for their everyday work—what has to be done, quality standards, customers' complaints, etc., e.g. a new procedure for ordering stock.

The method will vary, depending on the objective. Communication in organizations uses different media and addresses different-sized groups. Greenbaum summarized all this as shown in figure 14. Filling in a blank version of the grid can be an amusing and useful exercise to see what sorts of communication are most frequent in your own organization. It can be done in several ways. You can look at all the communication affecting one person over a week—for example, yourself, a colleague or someone new to the organization. What impression is this communication likely to give? Or you could look just at the written communication you receive. Is it mainly regulation? Another idea is to examine only the communication that had to do with integration. Is there very much? Alternatively you could try to collect examples for each of the squares in the grid. Which came most easily and which were found with most difficulty?

Let us now look at the process of communication for different sizes of audience and some of the difficulties that can be encountered.

Face to face

Think back over yesterday and ask how much of it you spent in communication. If you look at the different *types* of communication, I am sure you will find at least the following:

- Communication to achieve or obtain something. For example, persuading a customer to accept the off-specification material and to give it a try.

* Communication to get someone to behave in a particular way. For example, influencing a colleague to treat someone else sympathetically.
* Communication to find out or explain something. For example, finding out about the new directive from head office.
* Communication to express your feelings or to put yourself over in a particular way. For example, having a heated discussion, or a row, with a colleague.
* Communication to enjoy the companionship. For example, sharing a joke with the office.
* Communication to sort out a problem or ease a worry. For example, going and talking to the person in the next office and asking them what they are doing about it.
* Communication because you found it interesting. For example, talking to someone from another site, or organization, about their developments.
* Communication because the situation demanded it. For example, whilst waiting for a meeting to start.

Any or all of these can happen in a day. Indeed, several may occur in one conversation. We can see from the list that each of the different types of communication depends for completion on the two-way process. Only when the message is received and understood and the sender has feedback is the communication complete. Both the sender and the receiver have an active part to play. This process is sometimes called the 'communication chain', and systems (or information) theory terms are used to describe it.

For effective communication to take place each of the following stages has to be working well: encoding, transmitting, environment, receiving, decoding and feedback. Figure 15 shows how they are related and the sorts of checks one can make. Psychologists have made detailed experimental studies of this process.[2]

Encoding is the term used to describe the process of deciding what and how to communicate. The question of what to communicate is not as self-evident as it may appear. There are several questions that need asking. What is the purpose of the communication? Which will be the most influential points to make? The 'how' of the communication includes deciding who are the audience for it. What is their preferred style of message?

Figure 14
Organizational communication

		Regulation	Innovation	Integration	Information
Face to face (two)	Oral	Directions and requests	Superior/ subordinate ideas meet	Selection interview	Induction of new recruits
	Written	Job description and performance standards	Reports on visits, courses	Letter of welcome to new recruit	Memorandum
	Non-verbal	Gesture		Gesture	Demonstration of task to be performed
Small groups (three to ten)	Oral	Departmental meetings	Problem-solving meetings	Coffee break	Training groups
	Written	Agenda	Suggestions after meeting	Invitation to lunch	Works handbook
	Non-verbal	Pauses, silences	Seating arrangements	Meeting area conditions	Demonstration
Organiz-ation-wide	Oral	Meetings of department heads		Address to members of organization	Mass meeting
	Written	Organization chart	Suggestion scheme	House journals	Notice board
	Non-verbal	Style of office for organization member		House style in stationery, etc.	

Source: Based on H. W. Greenbaum, 'The audit of organizational communications', *Academy of Management Journal*, 1974, pp. 739–54.

Let us take as an imaginary example that I want you to go on a sales trip to Norway for a month. Are you someone who would leap at the opportunity or would you loathe being away from

Figure 15

The basic communications model or speech chain

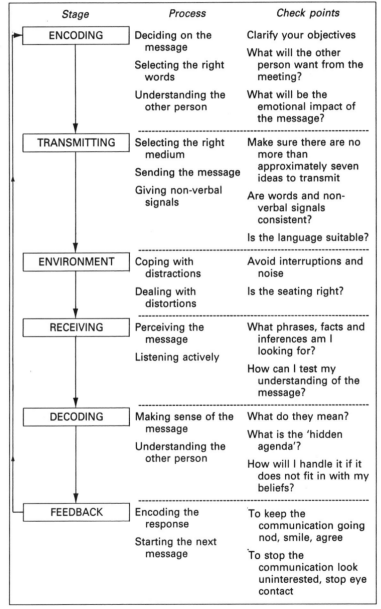

Stage	Process	Check points
ENCODING	Deciding on the message	Clarify your objectives
		What will the other person want from the meeting?
	Selecting the right words	
	Understanding the other person	What will be the emotional impact of the message?
TRANSMITTING	Selecting the right medium	Make sure there are no more than approximately seven ideas to transmit
	Sending the message	
	Giving non-verbal signals	Are words and non-verbal signals consistent?
		Is the language suitable?
ENVIRONMENT	Coping with distractions	Avoid interruptions and noise
	Dealing with distortions	Is the seating right?
RECEIVING	Perceiving the message	What phrases, facts and inferences am I looking for?
	Listening actively	
		How can I test my understanding of the message?
DECODING	Making sense of the message	What do they mean?
		What is the 'hidden agenda'?
	Understanding the other person	How will I handle it if it does not fit in with my beliefs?
FEEDBACK	Encoding the response	To keep the communication going nod, smile, agree
	Starting the next message	To stop the communication look uninterested, stop eye contact

Source: D. Torrington *and* J. Weightman, *Action Management*, London, Institute of Personnel Management, 1991.

home for so long? Should I emphasize the variety of places to be visited or the fact that the people mostly speak English? Do you prefer to be told things straight, or gently eased into the idea? *Transmitting* is the term used for the process of delivering the message. Sometimes it is appropriate to give the message in written form—for example, where it is a formal communication implying some sort of contract, such as agreed actions after a meeting, or a final warning over a disciplinary matter. Usually we prefer to communicate orally. Think how many times we try using the phone, even when we cannot get through, rather than resort to fax or letter. Trying to get the message in the most appropriate form for the audience is the great art of good communication. Continuing our example, would it be best to talk about Norway in a formally arranged meeting, in casual conversation or on the telephone?

Environment includes all the disruptions that can occur to a communication between the sender and the receiver: all the physical difficulties of other noise, technology breaking down or too great a distance between the communicators. There may be other hindrances such as inappropriate structure in the organization resulting in competing communications, or in the wrong person being communicated with. In our Norway example, you may mishear me if I am not usually the person to suggest such things. We might be frustrated by traffic noise, interruptions or a poor telephone line.

Receiving the message requires someone actually to hear or see it. This means being on the look-out for signals. So often a conversation is two people trying to get in with their own contribution rather than listening to the other's. Active listening is the process of trying to concentrate on the message. It requires that one is not uncomfortable physically nor trying to impose one's own views on the message. It also involves picking up on all the little clues like the non-verbal messages that might suggest something other than the words. You may not hear my message about Norway if I am too casual in my approach because you usually expect to hear that sort of thing more formally.

Decoding the message is trying to understand what it is that the other person is trying to communicate. A characteristic of how we organize our perceptions is that we use a 'frame of reference' to make sense of the incoming information: a personal set of ideas or attitudes that determine to some extent what we perceive in a particular situation. If the incoming message is not what we expect, or does not fit in with our frame of reference, we are likely to reject it. How easy it is for us to say that the other person is muddled or had misunderstood something when their message does not fit our view of things. It is much easier to hear messages we are ready to hear.

Continuing our example, do you believe what I am saying about Norway? Am I the sort of person who teases or winds people up? Am I always serious in what I say? What likelihood is there in your opinion that I would say this sort of thing truthfully?

Feedback is the loop that completes the communication process. Only when there is some acknowledgement of the message will the sender know whether it has been received in anything like the way that was intended. The feedback can be of several different kinds. Often it is just a non-verbal gesture, a smile or a laugh. Often it is by continuing the conversation. Sometimes it needs to be more formal. For example, a suggested tactic in interviews is to run through the interviewee's points to show you have understood them. Without feedback how can the sender know what has been received? In our example, I will only know if I have communicated about Norway if you say 'Yes, great,' or 'You're joking,' or 'No way,' or some such remark.

By understanding this communication chain we can more effectively adjust the nature of our communication to suit the varying communications we need to make at work. Look back to the eight types of communication listed at the beginning of this section and think what difference you would expect in the sequence, or chain, of each of them.

Small groups

The communication chain discussed above obviously applies to small groups as well as face-to-face interaction. For example, we have all experienced frustration when a pneumatic drill is going outside as we sit in a meeting on a hot afternoon, or the arrangement of chairs at a meeting prevents us from catching the eye of the chairperson. However, there are additional issues to consider for groups. (See also chapter 6, which describes the formal research material on communication in groups.)

One particular form of small-group communication is meetings.

Most managers attend a lot of meetings, and successful participation is important for influencing events. Meetings have both
overt and covert reasons for taking place. Communication about
these is both verbal and non-verbal. Some are given below.

Overt reasons for meetings:
• Making decisions: often prior discussions have arrived at the
  decisions and the meeting merely ratifies them.
• Making recommendations: to individuals or other groups.
• Training: newcomers to the group.
• Analysis and report: organizing material for another group.
• Information: this usually takes place under 'any other business'
  or 'matters arising'.

Covert reasons for meetings:
• Cohesion: feeling part of the whole by chatting beforehand,
  catching someone's eye or joking.
• Catharsis: giving vent to anger, even when nothing can be done.
• Manipulation: usually by senior staff.

Figure 16 is a check list developed to consider the arrangements
for regular meetings, to assist in running them effectively so that
the necessary communication can take place.

Organization-wide communication

Deciding the purpose of organization-wide communication is critical, as the opportunity for feedback is very limited in any but the
smallest organization. ACAS provide a helpful booklet[3] which lists
what should be communicated about the conditions of employment, the job and the organization by various face-to-face and
written methods.

We found that the purposes of organization-wide communication can be very varied. We examined whole-school briefing
meetings in secondary schools and found daily or weekly short
(five to ten-minute) briefing meetings quite common. They were
very effective at communicating information. They also helped
organizational cohesion, as they reinforced the personal identification of each member of staff with the community. They were
also useful as a 'trading floor', both before and after, as dates

could be arranged and deals struck. There were ritual celebrations, such as comings and goings. The school ethos was demonstrated by emphasizing priorities and endorsing certain norms. Reactions could be tested by any member of staff floating an idea to gauge the level of enthusiasm. Many other organizations could learn from these examples of practice in secondary schools.[4] In some organizations this type of meeting is called team briefing. It may be done at a unit, department or section level, depending on the size of the organization.

Collective bargaining is another form of whole-organization communication which takes place with a great deal of ritual and procedure. An understanding of the other side's point of view and political context is critical in reaching a conclusion. Often results come only when face-saving ways out can be found for both sides. The final public communication is often very carefully worded. See Friedman and Meredeen for an excellent account of a historic strike over equal pay at Ford.[5] Friedman was the senior convenor, Meredeen the industrial relations manager at the time.

Difficulties with organization-wide communication can occur for all the reasons given above in respect of face-to-face and group communication. Newsletters and video, which are commonly used in large organizations, can be effective for providing information but there is no feedback from the receiver. Barriers can also be due to the formal structures of the organization.[6] If the organization is very large, splitting the structure into relatively autonomous parts is likely to be more successful in assisting communication than increasing the amount of information. Where there are many different levels in the organization, communication becomes increasingly complex. Team briefing groups have been introduced to try to overcome some of these problems but eliminating a layer may be more effective in the long run. Hierarchy can also prevent some communication, because there is a social distance between people. Many junior employees will tell their boss only good news. One solution used by many managers is going 'walkabout' at a regular time. People find it easier to say things in familiar places, face-to-face and when it does not seem to be making a big issue out of it. Consequently the manager going walkabout finds out more and increases communication.

Figure 16

Check list. The questions can be used either in making arrangements for a regular meeting or for planning a particular session.

1. *Who has the right to attend?*
   Particular job holders?
   Their representatives?
   Anyone, so that no one feels excluded?

2. *What should the group consist of?*
   All those with the slightest interest?
   A smaller group to make discussion easier and more productive?
   Representatives of each layer in the hierarchy?
   A variety of personalities, to ensure a lively discussion?
   Consistent membership, to allow the group to mature?
   Only those with expertise in this area?

3. *What is the brief or terms of reference of the meeting?*
   Does the meeting have the power to take a decision?
   Can the meeting make a recommendation?
   How wide can the discussion usefully range?
   Is there a decision relating to this topic already made that cannot be changed?
   Are there some conclusions that would be unacceptable? To whom?

4. *What is the agenda of this meeting?*
   What do we need to consider?
   Is there too much here?
   Who has access to putting items on the agenda?
   Which order should things come in?
   Who gets a copy?
   Will 'matters arising' and 'any other business' take up a lot of time?

5. *What about the physical location and arrangements?*
   Have we identified a room, and does everyone know which it is?
   Can everyone see everyone else and make eye contact?
   Is there something to write on?
   Is it noisy, hot, cold, liable to interruptions?
   Can everyone get there in the time allowed?

6. *Who makes a contribution?*
   Who has something to say?
   How can I keep the longwinded brief?

How can I get the time to contribute?
When should I nudge the meeting towards a decision/the
  next item?
How will individuals indicate that they want a turn?

7. *Minutes or report of the meeting*
  Who writes them?
  Should they just list the actions decided and the name
    of the person responsible?
  Is it important to describe the discussion and issues?
  Who gets a copy?
  Do people other than participants or regular circulation
    receive a copy if they are affected by an issue
    discussed (e.g. caretaker)?
  What will be the effect of the minutes on those people
    who attended/did not attend?
  Who are we trying to influence with these minutes?

8. *Implementation of proposals*
  Who has agreed to do what?
  How can we help each other to get on with it?
  Who else can we involve?
  How can we monitor the implementation?
  Do we need a review date?
  What can I do to get things moving?

9. *Calendar of future meetings*
  How often do we need to meet?
  Could sub-groups meet?
  What other meetings do the members have to attend?
  Do we want a regular time or do we wait until we have
    an agenda?
  Is our cycle of need different from the norm?

10. *And finally . . .*
  Is the meeting really necessary or could we use our time
    better?
  Is a meeting the best way of achieving the declared
    objectives?

Source: D. P. Torrington *and* J. Weightman, *Management and organization in secondary schools*, Hemel Hempstead, Simon & Schuster, 1989.

The barriers to effective communication

Communication failure happens when someone is unable to transmit the desired message to another. A failure to understand often lies at the root of conflict because different needs, interests and experiences have not been communicated. Neither party has been able to understand the situation from the other person's point of view. Communication can fail in three main ways:

- Ineffective sending.
- Ineffective reception.
- A mismatch between the communicators.

Let us look at each in turn.

Ineffective *sending* may be due to the person having an inadequate vocabulary, being inarticulate, or being inhibited because they are nervous. It may also be due to incorrect assumptions about the receiver. How often people assume the listener has the knowledge when he has not, or are insensitive to the experience of the person being addressed.

Ineffective *reception* may be due to a sensory disability such as partial hearing or to the attention of the receiver being distracted. If the communication comes too quickly or in too large a chunk the receiver may be overloaded. The input may also get distorted by the receiver's expectations, personality or assumptions about what is going on.

Mismatch between communicators occurs where they do not share the same language, non-verbal conventions, concepts or capacity for relating the concepts. The most obvious example is trying to communicate with someone in another language which you do not speak. Closer to home, we may feel uncomfortable in someone's presence because they prefer to keep a greater, or lesser, distance when speaking than we do.

So far all these issues have been about interpersonal communication. There are also barriers due to the *environment* in which the communication takes place. Obvious physical barriers are noise, distance and the limitations of technology. When the telephone system breaks down at work every effort is made to get it working as soon as possible. Other problems may be less obvious, such as the layout of the office. For example, open-plan offices are often introduced with the idea that they will improve communication between people in the same section or department. Sometimes this is so, but I have visited several open-plan offices where the introduction of large plants and hat stands is a sign that people are seeking more privacy. People frequently complain about having to listen to others' conversations. The arrangement of chairs by a table suggests different types of interaction. For example, sitting face-to-face is most appropriate during negotiations; sitting round a corner at ninety degrees is appropriate for a problem-solving session; side-by-side suggests a co-operative exercise.

Implications for managers

Communication is the lifeblood of human interaction. Think how much more difficult it is to get to know a deaf person as compared with a blind person. Inevitably communication is never perfect, as we do not understand each other perfectly and so sometimes we communicate the wrong thing. However, we can make some efforts towards more effective communication.

Communication between members of an organization and those outside it is not properly the subject of managing human resources. But clearly some of the ideas of effective communication within organizations outlined here are equally appropriate elsewhere. This may imply such things as communicating with school leavers about recruitment opportunities, where thinking about their perspective will be crucial. Or communicating with customers about a price change: should it be done face-to-face or by letter? How much communication with the local community about waste disposal is appropriate?

Communication is often blamed for organizational and personal problems. Often the communication can be improved. It may also be that the 'what', 'to whom', 'by whom', 'using which media?' or 'in what context?' is to blame. There are other concepts besides communication to analyse these problems such as organization structure, managing generally, setting objectives clearly. It is always worth unravelling a communication difficulty to see what are the various factors affecting the communication.

Summary statements for managers

- Not everything called a problem of communication is due to communication difficulties. It may be other aspects of the organization that are at fault.
- Communication in organizations can be about regulation, innovation, integration and information.
- Communication takes place only when the chain from sender to receiver is completed with feedback to the sender.
- Meetings are a critical part of managers' communication and it is worth spending time getting them right.

References

1 H. W. GREENBAUM, 'The audit of organizational communications'. *Academy of Management Journal*, 1974, pp. 739–54.
2 See, for example, U. NEISSER, *Cognitive psychology*. New York, Appleton-Century-Crofts, 1966, and D. I. SLOBIN, *Psycholinguistics*. Glenville, Ill., Scott Foresman, 1971, for detailed studies. A more readable reference is H. J. LEAVITT, *Managerial psychology*, fourth edition. Chicago, University of Chicago Press, 1978.
3 Advisory Conciliation and Arbitration Service, *Workplace communications*. London, ACAS, 1985.
4 D. P. TORRINGTON and J. B. WEIGHTMAN, *Management and organization in secondary schools: training materials*. Hemel Hempstead, Simon & Schuster, 1989.
5 H. FRIEDMAN and S. MEREDEEN, *The dynamics of industrial conflict: lessons from Ford*. London, Croom Helm, 1980.
6 For details of organizational structures see the books in this series by D. FARNHAM, *The corporate environment* and M. ARMSTRONG, *Management processes and functions*. London, Institute of Personnel Management, 1990.

8

The Informal Organization

A common view of organizations is that they are formal, precise structures of co-ordinated human activity.

> What you may expect to see—but don't—is an animated organization chart—a pyramid of little boxes, each sitting astride seven others, and seven more under each of those seven, and seven more, and so on. Perhaps, too, you expect to see each of the top boxes occupied by a faceless figure in a gray flannel uniform and the lower boxes occupied by figures, also faceless, in overalls. Each figure is busily pushing levers to make other figures turn and jump in unison until the whistle blows, when they all stop together.[1]

Some people will see this as a description of perfection: for others it is a nightmare. What is certain is that no organization works so mechanically in practice. Where such precision is attempted it proves ineffective, because people are not uniform in abilities or experience. Nor are they willing to be constrained to fit neatly into little boxes. Another difficulty with rigid organizations is they have proved least able to change, adapt to new challenges or seize the opportunities offered by new technologies. This chapter is about the importance for managers of understanding the informal ways of getting things done in organizations. Most managing is not of a formal nature.

Organization culture

There has been a move in management circles away from an emphasis on formal procedures and structures as the most important organizing devices of organizations. There is increasing emphasis on the organization's culture, that is, its characteristic spirit and beliefs. This is often called the organization climate. Culture is seen in the way people treat each other, the nature of working relationships and the normal attitude to change. In other words, the values and norms of the organization are manifestations of its culture. It is these features of organizational life that are likely to have more effect on people's behaviour than formal reporting relationships or procedures.

Understanding organization culture can be useful in two ways. First, if you understand what the culture of an organization is you can work with it rather than against it. This will enable you to get things done more easily. Second, you can try to change an unproductive culture and make it more appropriate to the current situation by trying to manage the culture. There are several examples of organizations which have made great efforts to move away from being bound by precedent, inward-looking, with strong feelings of 'them and us', alienation and lack of commitment. The new culture usually emphasizes such values as service to the customer, innovation, consensus and co-operation. Examples are British Airways and the leading retail companies. However not all culture management has been as successful and often a strong unitarist culture has been attempted.

What, then, is organization culture? C. Handy examines four varieties of organization culture, with their respective structures and systems.[2] Each type varies in the way authority is exercised, how far ahead they plan, the way people dress, whether decisions are taken by committees or individuals, and the nature of the buildings in which they work. The four types of culture are as follows.

1 *The power culture* is often found in small, entrepreneurial organizations. It depends on a central, all-powerful head. The structure is best seen as a web (see figure 17). Influence and power spread out from the centre on a line of personal contact. There are few rules and systems, but often precedent is followed. Such cultures have the ability to move quickly and react well to threat or danger. Size is a problem, as a web cannot support too many activities, something that a small company has to bear in mind as it expands. The quality of the central figure or figures is critical, and succession is often a problematic issue. A web without a spider has no strength.

2 *The role culture* is found in large bureaucracies. It depends on rational and logical arrangements. It has a structure like a Greek temple (see figure 17). The pillars are the functional specialisms, with a co-ordinating top management represented by the

pediment. The emphasis is on the role of particular jobs, not on the individual who fills the role. It is most successful in a stable environment, a monopoly, long product life, or where the market is stable. Successful examples have been the civil service, the oil industry and retail banking. It becomes insecure, when things change.

3 *The task culture* is a job or project oriented organization. The emphasis is on getting things done. It is best represented by a net (see figure 17). Influence is based on expertise, and most people working in this type of organization expect to have some sort of expertise. It is very much based on teams of people working together. An example would be a television company, where individuals from different professions work together on a particular production and then disperse. This style works well for quick adaptation to change but has difficulty developing economies of scale or great depth of expertise. Control can be difficult, particularly when resources are tight.

4 *The person culture* is far less common than the others. The individual is the central point. The structure and systems are there to serve him. Examples are professional partnerships, families or barristers' chambers. A cluster best represents it (see figure 17). Systems and procedures can be introduced only by common consent. Few organizations of this sort exist, but many people hold the ideal. Specialists in other types of organization often take this view: they can be difficult to manage, as they can always move elsewhere.

Handy continues his analysis by explaining that most large organizations will have different cultures operating in different parts of the structure. For example, head office may well be a power culture for top managers with a person culture for the specialists. The manufacturing plants may well be operating with a role culture when the research unit is basically a task culture. Only by understanding these differences can one influence events in appropriate ways.

Peters and Waterman's book *In Search of Excellence*[3] has undoubtedly been the most influential management book of the last decade. The authors set out to examine the most successful American companies and the basis of their success. The conclusion was that it was the nature of the culture that determined success and that the 'excellent' companies had several things in common. Peters and Waterman give seven formulas for excellence.

1 *A bias towards action.* The successful organization is not obsessed with analysis or formal procedures and decision-making. It has lots of practical and pragmatic devices that counteract the stultification that often comes with size. The task of senior management is problem-finding, not problem-solving, which is delegated to others. It means looking for opportunities for the organization to be better. Another aspect of the bias to action is ability to control things after the event rather than before it. This means 'Try it and see if it works', not asking permission for everything.

2 *Close to the customer.* Getting things right for the customer, not the profit statement, is the driving force. Casual conversation tends to be about the product. Time is spent talking to customers, listening to them and finding out what they want. This also involves identifying precisely who your customers are. No one can satisfy everyone all the time.

3 *Autonomy and entrepreneurship.* The 'excellent' companies had many leaders and innovators. Communication and ideas were encouraged. Failure was not penalized if something could be learned from it. Trying is the essential thing; succeeding is a bonus.

4 *Productivity through people.* Trusting people is the key. This means getting away from such things as time clocks and attendance registers; being prepared to give people confidential information; asking for ideas and treating them as adults. It is trust at the expense of control.

5 *Hands-on, value-driven.* The basic philosophy of an organization has more to do with its achievements than with technological or economic resources. The philosophy must be lived, not just voiced, by the top people. It may be quality, service, openness or honesty. This involves transforming energies into a common purpose and has given rise to the phrase 'transforming leadership'.

6 *Stick to the knitting.* The organizations that lost their way were those which tried to do too many things. The ones that stuck to their core task and did not become distracted from it were the ones that succeeded. The realization has led to businesses shedding many of their peripheral activities, such as canteens and transport, not just getting back to their basic business activity.

7 *Simple form, lean staff.* Complicated structures and many-layered hierarchies do not produce excellent organizations. As few people at the centre as possible, seems to be the message.

These terms have become commonplace in management discussion. Several companies have deliberately tried to adopt such

Figure 17
Forms of organization

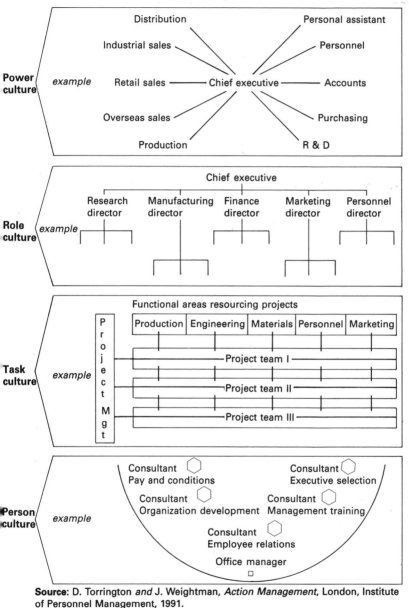

Source: D. Torrington *and* J. Weightman, *Action Management,* London, Institute of Personnel Management, 1991.

practices. The phrases have also become commonplace in studies of organizations.[4] Trying to change the culture of an organization is a very difficult process. There is a good deal of advice around: perhaps the most penetrating analysis of organizational culture is by E. H. Schein.[5] He distinguishes two sorts of mechanisms for organizational change, primary and secondary. The primary mechanisms of culture change are:

* What leaders pay most attention to.
* How leaders react to crises and critical incidents.
* Role modelling, teaching and coaching by leaders.
* Criteria for allocating rewards and determining status.
* Criteria for selection, promotion and termination.

The first three emphasize the importance of leading by example. All are about the leader showing people what matters. The second two are to do with emphasizing people as individuals. Those who fit in or help the kind of organization that is wanted are selected and rewarded; those who do not are not.

The secondary mechanisms for the articulation and reinforcement of culture are:[6]

* The organizational structure.
* Systems and procedures.
* Space, buildings and facades.
* Stories and legends about important events and people.
* Formal statements of philosophy and policy.

These secondary mechanisms are the formal aspect of management and organization. Interestingly they have been the traditional areas of study and training for managers, partly because they are easier to write about than the messy business of leadership and people. In Schein's view they still have a place but as support to the more important aspects of showing people what is important and recognizing those who demonstrate desired behaviour. Note that the formal statements come second. It is the *in*formal aspects of the organization which are seen to be the more powerful in influencing people's behaviour.

Culture has become a much discussed term in management circles in the last decade. It is worth spending some time thinking about your own organization to see whether it fits into any of

Handy's or Peters and Waterman's categories. For those who have only ever worked in one organization it is worth arranging a visit to another just to see how differently everyday things—from how the day starts, or mail distribution, to security—are dealt with.

Networks

As organizations become less formal, with people less dependent on clear, hierarchical relationships, there is greater emphasis on everyone, and particularly managers, developing and maintaining extensive networks of personal contacts. John Kotter has described networks as a reflection of the political activity of managers.[7] The individual manager identifies a large number of people both inside and outside the organization, who can help in getting things done. It may be in providing information, speeding something through, getting round the system, chasing something up, supporting an item at a meeting, checking a piece of information, altering a date, arranging a meeting or doing a favour. Kotter found that the general managers he studied had very large networks of contacts, sometimes running to thousands, and every relationship was different. It included current and previous colleagues, the boss's boss and the subordinates' subordinates, customers, suppliers, members of professional bodies, and so on.

Networks are personal, not hierarchical. Clearly the job title you have will determine some of your network, but much of the effectiveness of a network depends on individual expertise and social skill. People are more likely to assist if they feel you are able to complement their knowledge and ability in some way, believe the request is legitimate and worthwhile, and respect or like you. Networks are the way members of an organization share ideas, information, resources and assistance. They are not the same as the 'old boy' system, which protects self-interest and can create gender differences. For example, women may feel excluded from the informal business contact which takes place in the pub or on the golf course.

Power and authority

As organizations increasingly depend on less formal forms of influence it becomes increasingly important for managers to understand power and the use of it. Those who understand the subtleties of power in relationships are better able to get things done than those who ignore them.

> The graveyards of history are strewn with the corpses of reformers who failed to reform anything, or revolutionaries who failed to win power . . . of anti-revolutionaries who failed to prevent a revolution—men and women who failed not only because of the forces arrayed against them but because the pictures in their minds about power and influence were simplistic and inaccurate.[8]

The formal structure of an organization is a map of official working relationships and has been the main device for formally distributing power amongst its members. It has, however, never been the only source of power in organizations (see figure 18). Most importantly, position power has always needed to be supported by something else, usually resource power.

Very often in organizations ideas about power and authority are encompassed in the idea of credibility. People with high credibility are worthy of belief, trustworthy, convincing and respected. They are listened to and can get people to do things willingly, whereas their colleagues who lack credibility meet resistance and have to rely on formal means of getting things done. The difficulty for managers is that they often have to maintain credibility with several different constituencies. To remain effective it is important that credibility is earned and sustained with those working in the same department or unit. It is only by keeping in sight of the main tasks and retaining a down-to-earth quality that we can ensure that new ideas are based on reality and that there is a ready-made network to put changes into practice.

A useful distinction is drawn between two sorts of authority. A. Carter distinguishes the two types as '*in* authority' and '*an* authority'.[9] The first, which implies having a position of authority, requires support, whereas the latter stands on its own. Being *an* authority means having the skill, knowledge and expertise that others consult willingly. In our own research on middle managers[10] we found that credibility within units was dependent on being an

Figure 18
Sources of power

1. **Position**
   Resources Control access to what others need; whether subordinates, peers or superiors. It includes the following: materials, information, rewards, finance, time, staff, promotion, references.

   Delegation Whether jobs are pushed down the hierarchy; with rights of veto retained or not.

   Gatekeeper Control information, relax or tighten rules, make life difficult or easy depending on loyalty of individuals.

2. **Expertise**
   Skill Being an expert. Having a skill others need or desire.

   Uncertainty Those who have expertise to deal with a crisis become powerful till it is over.

   Indispensable Either through expertise or being an essential part of the administrative process.

3. **Personal qualities**
   Motivation Some seek power more enthusiastically than others.

   Physical prowess Being bigger or stronger than others... Not overtly used in management except as controller of resources. However, statistically leaders tend to be taller than the led.

   Charisma Very rare indeed. Much discussed in early management literature as part of leadership qualities, but usually control of resources can account for claims of charismatic power.

   Persuasion skills Bargaining and personal skills that enable one to make the most of one's other powers, such as resources.

4. **Political factors**
   Debts Having others under obligation for past favours.

   Control of agenda Coalition and other techniques for managing how the issues are, or are not, presented. Being present when important decisions are taken, control of minutes.

   Dependence Where one side depends on the other for willing co-operation, the power of removal exists. Strikes, or threatening to resign *en bloc* are two examples.

Source: D. P. Torrington *and* J. B. Weightman, *The reality of school management*, Oxford, Blackwells, 1989.

authority on the unit's main function, whether it was telecommunications, selling, engineering, purchasing, flying aircraft or educating children. Managers who lose touch with their expertise are in danger of losing credibility with their colleagues and consequently will have difficulty getting things done.

Power and authority in organizations depend also on legitimacy. We have only as much power and authority as those we seek to exert them over will allow us. Various devices are used within organizations to legitimize power and authority. The formal organization charts, job titles and pay structures are one such device. Another is the demonstration of leadership. Western society, and its organizations with it, have developed a taste for informal means of legitimizing power and authority. So it has become increasingly important for managers to come to terms with credibility, which is often all about establishing legitimate power and authority. Winning commitment from others is also a phrase used to describe this. For those who cannot demonstrate a technical authority credibility is often based on such personal qualities as willingness to do things, working hard and demonstrating enthusiasm.

The manager who builds and sustains a network of contacts and has maintained credibility with colleagues is more likely to be able to consult them about new projects effectively. They in turn are more likely to hear and understand if things start going wrong rather than having to wait till it is too late. The manager who relies on formal relationships and lacks credibility will only be told what they expect to hear and only when they *have* to be told.

Implications for managers

It is often thought that being a good manager is all about setting up procedures and control systems; you then measure how well these have been complied with to test whether your management has been 'good'. The procedures and controls often meet with hostility and resentment from others, who comply reluctantly and inefficiently. Commonly even more control devices are introduced because managing has been interpreted as controlling other people. This is a dangerously narrow view of the management process. Handy describes well what happens if it is carried out:

> ... morale is lowered, secrecy and subversion mount, energy and commitment reduce. Lonely and anxious, management then too often responds with more controls and checks, more assumed rights. Self-fulfilling, the organization begins to respond only to whips and spurs and everyone wonders what went wrong.[11]

Some control is welcomed by everyone, so that things can be done in an orderly manner. Deciding what to control is the important issue. Most people find control of behaviour oppressive. Control of activities is often seen as taking away all the interest in a job, whereas control of the outputs is seen as acceptable and a legitimate part of management's responsibility. Controlling the 'what' may be a job for management but the 'how' can be delegated.

The other side of the coin is autonomy, that is, allowing people to decide for themselves how and what to do. As control slackens autonomy increases. It may be individual autonomy or groups deciding together. Allowing others to take decisions and implement them is not easy for the manager. It means giving up some power. Equally it is not easy for those who have been trained to be dependent. Where staff have not been trusted in the past they may be uncertain how to react. Training, careful management and patience will be needed. Only by practice will people learn how to take decisions and accept responsibility. The advice is not to give up at the first unsuccessful attempt.

The informal organization we have discussed in this chapter seems to be associated with really getting things done. Managers have to interpret their role as being about control only to a limited extent. The difficulty is that in the past many managers' power has rested on control of resources, monitoring systems, agenda and so on. It is not easy to relinquish this part of their work. However, if power is based on expertise, then managers will be more influential in the organization. The expertise has to be in something that others will find useful – an expertise in underwater knitting, if unusual, does not make one very influential in most organizations. In the past a claim to management expertise was sought in order to enhance management power. Now it is not sufficient to claim expertise, it needs to be demonstrated. There are several kinds of expertise for managers to develop. The most obvious is technical expertise in the organization's product. Another is a transferable expertise such as systems analysis. For others there is the expertise of really knowing how the place works, based on years of experience and personal contact.

The art for managers is to ensure that they are developing in themselves, and in those they are responsible for, a suitable range of expertise. This will enable people to contribute enthusiastically and with increasing autonomy. At the same time managers need to control the few central issues. In this way the informal organization can be a productive and satisfying place to work.

Summary statements for managers

- The way people treat each other and the nature of working relationships vary from organization to organization. Trying to understand the particular culture of an organization makes it easier to get things done.
- Excellent companies appear to have seven things in common. Most importantly, they have a bias to action, are close to the customer and encourage autonomy.
- Large networks of mutually supportive contacts are an important part of getting through the agenda of things that need doing.
- Power and authority are important issues for managers to understand if they want to influence people and events.

References

1 H. J. LEAVITT, W. R. DILL and H. B. EYRING, *The organizational world*, New York, Harcourt Brace Jovanovich, 1973.
2 C. HANDY, *Understanding organizations*, second edition. Harmondsworth, Penguin Books, 1985.
3 T. J. PETERS and R. H. WATERMAN, *In search of excellence*. London, Harper & Row, 1982.
4 See P. MARSH, P. BARWISE, K. THOMAS and R. WENSLEY, *Managing strategic investment decisions in large diversified companies*. London, London Business School, 1988, and British Institute of Management, *The responsive organisation*. London, BIM, 1989, for two British ones.
5 E. H. SCHEIN, *Organizational culture and leadership*. San Francisco, Jossey Bass, 1985, pp. 224–37.
6 *Ibid.*, 237–42.
7 J. KOTTER, *The general managers*. New York, Free Press, 1982.
8 R. DAHL, *Modern political analysis*, second edition. Englewood Cliffs, N. J., Prentice Hall, 1970, p. 15.
9 A. CARTER, *Authority and democracy*. London, Allen & Unwin, 1979.
10 D. TORRINGTON and J. B. WEIGHTMAN, 'Middle management work'. *Journal of General Management*, 1987.
11 C. HANDY, 'The organisations of consent', in *The changing university*, ed. D. Piper and R. Glatter. Windsor, National Foundation for Educational Research, 1977.

PART III

Managing People in the Organization

9

Finding and Selecting People

Part III of this book deals with specific issues of managing people in organizations. It is addressed to line managers, in a variety of situations. All the issues covered are the responsibility of line managers. However, personnel managers, personnel departments, human resource managers and human resource departments will be sources of advice about all of them. These specialists are also expected to provide policy, systems and guidelines within organizations on all these issues for individual managers to follow and use.

Many managers fantasize about selecting the ideal team to work in their department or unit. We all imagine we would work better if we had just the right colleagues. However, this is possible only when a new unit is being set up. The reality for most people is they have to manage those who are already in post when they take on the job, with the possibility of recruiting additional or replacement staff later.

Some management jobs do involve a great deal of selecting people to come and work in the organization. Hotel managers are frequently looking for chambermaids and kitchen porters. Managers in high-tech. industries, such as flight simulation, spend a lot of time travelling the country interviewing possible candidates and trying to persuade them to join. Many organizations have full-time recruiters who try to ensure a constant supply of suitable employees—for example, the high-street banks have a number of people recruiting at graduate and non-graduate level full-time. Other managers rarely have the opportunity to select people to work with them. For example, educational establishments often have very stable staff; and managers who work on their own or in a small team obviously will not select others so often.

Not all selection is of people new to the organization. For many managers the only selection they are involved with is from internal candidates. In large organizations, such as an oil company or the civil service, when a vacancy occurs it is usually filled from within.

Initial selection to the company is of young people and dealt with centrally, so that individual managers may be involved in this initial selection only peripherally, by showing people around.

Overview of manpower planning

Every organization needs to have some idea of what sort of people, and how many, it is going to need in the future. This process is called manpower planning. There are various questions associated with it. Is there some new project planned? How many and what sort of people will be needed to do the work? Who is getting near retirement age, and how shall we be able to replace their expertise? Do we need to start training someone up now? What is the age range in our department, unit or organization? Does it mean that in ten years' time there will be too many chiefs and not enough indians? Or will we all have retired? Will the current plans for investment in new machinery mean we need fewer people in the future? If so, how are we going to manage the reduction? What sort of skills are we going to need? Do we need to make some changes to the skills mix in some departments? Are there savings to be made by not using skilled people to do unskilled work? These questions, and many others, are put together with the future plans of the organization and a manpower plan is developed.

The main objective of manpower planning is to interpret the company's forecasts, such as production and sales, in terms of manpower requirements. Another objective is to indicate what manpower constraints there may be on company policy in the future, for example, shortage of trained personnel, a new local employer, changes in the rules applicable to part-time employees. Manpower planning is normally a specialist's task, undertaken within the personnel function, but it involves the following processes.

First, it is necessary to convert the plans, objectives and commitments of the organization into manpower requirements. Second, detailed information about current employees needs to be collected. This includes ages, jobs, training and turnover. Third, an analysis of the possible supply of people from outside is useful. After this has been done several sorts of discussions can result. Do we need to improve our utilization of people by looking at job efficiency, productivity and manning levels? Do we need to improve our manpower policies with regard to pay and benefits, training or recruitment? Is there a long-term problem that we can start working on now?

With the predicted reduction of young people coming on to the labour market in the 1990s compared with the 1980s, organizations will need to think about whether these manpower plans can involve the retraining of established staff and the employment of older staff more than has been usual in the past. The manpower plan requires frequent adaptation as circumstances change but will be the central reference point for decisions about recruiting and selecting staff. This involves decisions both about newcomers and about new jobs for established staff.

The systematic approach to recruitment

An appropriate recruitment system needs to be set up in every organization so that for each new recruit a routine exists which can be monitored. The system needs to be effective in producing enough suitable candidates, cost-effective and fair. It would usually be the responsibility of the personnel department.[1]

When a vacancy occurs several questions need to be asked. Do we want the same job to be done, or have there been changes? Do we anticipate any changes in the job in the foreseeable future? Are we going to reorganize the work of this section soon? When such questions have been answered the next step is writing a job description which defines the work and responsibilities of the job.

ACAS suggest that a good *job description* can be drawn up if the following points are remembered:

> *Main purpose of job*—try to describe this in one sentence; if you cannot find a main purpose, perhaps the whole job needs reviewing.
>
> *Main tasks of the job*—always use active verbs, like 'writing', 'filing', 'milling', 'repairing', to describe precisely what is done, rather than vague terms such as 'in charge of ', 'deals with'.
>
> *Scope of the job*—although the 'main tasks' describe what is done, they don't necessarily indicate the scope or importance

Figure 19
Person specifications

The Seven-point Plan
1. *Physical make-up:* health, appearance, bearing and speech.
2. *Attainments:* education, qualifications, experience.
3. *General intelligence:* intellectual capacity.
4. *Special aptitudes:* mechanical, manual dexterity, facility in use of words and figures.
5. *Interests:* intellectual, practical, constructional, physically active, social, artistic.
6. *Disposition:* acceptability, influence over others, steadiness, dependability, self-reliance.
7. *Circumstances:* any special demands of the job, such as ability to work unsocial hours, travel abroad, etc.

The Five-fold Grading System
1. *Impact on others:* physical make-up, appearance, speech and manner.
2. *Acquired qualifications:* education, vocational training, work experience.
3. *Innate abilities:* quickness of comprehension and aptitude for learning.
4. *Motivation:* individual goals, consistency and determination in following them up, success rate.
5. *Adjustment:* emotional stability, ability to stand up to stress and ability to get on with people.

Source: Based on A. Rodger, *The seven-point plan*, London, National Institute of Industrial Psychology, 1952, and J. Munro Fraser, *Employment interviewing*, London, Macdonald and Evans, 1950.

of the job. This can be done by describing the value of equipment or materials handled, the degree of precision required, and the number of people supervised, etc.[2]

You might also want to list the main duties of the job holder. The job description not only helps with recruitment but can also suggest ways of inducting and training the newcomer.

Once you have a job description it is possible to draw up a *person specification*. This describes the knowledge, skills and abilities that an ideal candidate would have. Two well established classifications exist to help this process, Rodger's Seven-point Plan and Munro Fraser's Five-fold Grading System (see figure 19).[3] For jobs where lists of competencies, see next chapter for more details, exist these can be very useful for drawing up a person specification. The important thing is to set appropriate levels for these character-

Figure 20

Methods of recruiting candidates

Internal advertising
Word of mouth
Local schools and colleges
Local newspapers, radio, TV and cinemas
Job centres
Trade unions
Commercial employment agencies
National newspapers
Specialist and professional papers
Recruitment consultants
Executive search organizations or 'head hunters'
Recruitment fairs
Professional and executive recruitment
University appointment boards
The Officers' Association

istics for the particular job. Too high a specification may leave no suitable candidates, too low a specification may underestimate the problems associated with the job being done badly. Decisions then need to be taken about the terms and conditions associated with the job.

Different *recruitment methods* are available for attracting suitable candidates. The best is that which produces a suitable candidate at the least cost. Figure 20 lists some of the methods available. The personnel department will usually deal with the administration involved in using them but line managers need to make their needs clear. The personnel department will also help draw up the advertisement and the press will help with layout if necessary. Similarly, the personnel department will usually have a standard application form to send to prospective candidates which then becomes the basis of the personnel record for the successful candidate. The line manager needs to decide whether there is any other information personnel need to know for selection to start.

Selection techniques and their efficacy

The complexity of the job to be filled will be reflected in the nature of the selection process. For a straightforward job a short interview and perhaps a simple test may be all that is required. For other jobs a more varied strategy may be called for. Some of these are listed below.[4] Whichever methods are used, it is important that the immediate supervisor is involved in the decision. This will ensure that the supervisor is committed to welcoming the new worker, and the candidate will have the opportunity of deciding whether they can work for the supervisor.

Selection tests. These are tests of attainment and of performance related to the skills necessary to do the job. A typical example is a typing test for secretaries. It is important that the test really tries skills that are used in the job and does not discriminate unfairly. For example, it might be reasonable for a garage to test applicants for a mechanic's job by examining a car engine but unreasonable for them to test them on a vintage car that only the owner's son would be likely to be familiar with. Selection tests need to be selected very carefully, as many are either out of date or not specifically related to the job that needs doing.

Group selection. There are different types: group problem-solving, command exercises, leaderless groups. These have been developed to assess candidates' ability to get on with other people and influence them. They have been used for management selection where people feel that interview alone is insufficient. For example, a local authority selecting the deputy head of a secondary school had each of the candidates run a discussion group with five members of staff about how to introduce a new teaching method. The candidates felt aggrieved when they all interpreted the situation differently. Group selection is time-consuming and expensive, and hence appropriate only where social leadership is required.

Psychological tests. These have proved controversial but are used by many organizations in the UK. They can be tests of general intelligence, special aptitudes, motivation, attitudes or personality. For example, the Ordnance Survey may test candidates wanting to become surveyors for visual acuity and spatial abilities. It is important that they are used only by trained people, and they are most effective with young people who have less of a track record.

References are frequently used in the public sector. Their main purpose is to confirm information and opinions formed elsewhere. They should be taken up only with the candidates' permission. The practice of asking for them on application forms can make applicants nervous, particularly where the present employer is named. References should really only be used to confirm a decision that has already been taken, as they so often tell you more about the person who has written the reference than the one it is about. Usually the conventions of format make it necessary to read between the lines. There is, of course, the additional problem that someone's current boss may write a good reference to get rid of them or a bad one so they will not leave!

Assessment centres. Larger companies increasingly use this method, where a number of short-listed candidates undergo a range of selection techniques, including group exercises. It has the value that a variety of evidence is collected and a balanced assessment is possible. The difficulty is the expense in time and money, which can be justified only if you expect the successful candidate to make a significant contribution to the organization.

The selection interview

The interview is the main method used for selecting people. Whenever research is done into selection interviews their reliability and validity are found to be highly variable.[5] Yet we all still prefer to select and be selected by interview. Why is this?

One of the important aspects is the actual ritual of having the interview.

> The selection interview is at least partly an initiation rite, not as elaborate as entry to commissioned rank in the armed forces, not as whimsical as finding one's way into the Brownie ring, but still a process of going through hoops and being found worthy.[6]

Part of the ritual is that interviews are the point at which the whole recruitment and selection process reaches its climax. All the information about the candidate and all those involved in making the decision come together at a predetermined time and place. People may meet the candidate separately, in pairs or together, but they will regroup to discuss the outcome afterwards. This is the ritual associated with 'being the organization'. The rite of initiation into the organization is ignored at one's peril. So how can one get the best results from selection interviews? Unless your organization has a specific, structured, interview schedule here is a sequence which can be used for selection interviewing.

Preparation is important. First, examine your person specification and compare the applicants with it. What do you need to ask more questions about: their experience, their qualifications? Second, plan what questions you are going to ask. They can be about the candidate's knowledge, ability and attitudes but should be related to the job and not due merely to personal curiosity. Third, what are the candidates likely to ask about? What information will you need to answer them? Fourth, look after the housekeeping. Ensure you have a suitable room, that you will not be interrupted, and that Reception know where to send the candidates. What you are aiming to do is to select someone fairly, having given them the opportunity to understand what the job involves.

Conducting the interview is about trying to achieve a suitable balance between formality and friendliness. It is helpful to begin by describing what is going to happen—this will include introducing all those present—and when it will finish. Start with questions about aspects where it will be relatively easy for the candidate to reply. For example, what do they do in their present job—going through their career chronologically. The flow of the interview is the interviewer's responsibility. It can be nudged in the right direction by encouraging phrases such as 'I was particularly interested in . . .' or discouraging ones like 'I would prefer it if we could move on to exploring . . .' The use of gesture and other non-verbal signs such as eye contact or nods will keep the interviewee directed on to the subjects you want to explore. It is worth keeping some brief notes openly during the interview as memory-jogs for later. Towards the end ask the candidate if they have any questions, and be ready to answer them. At the end, tell them the terms and conditions of the job and when they can expect to hear the result. Ensure that someone sorts out travel expenses, conducts a tour of the workplace and sees the candidate to the door.

Afterwards you need to *make notes* of your impressions immediately. You need to consider to what extent the candidate meets your specification. Refer back to the person specification and compare strengths and weaknesses. Ask yourself to what extent the career pattern shows progress and development appropriate to the job. When you have made your decision, consulting others where appropriate, inform all those interviewed of the outcome. Start planning for the newcomer's arrival.

Panel interviews are a special case of selection interviewing. All the above good practice applies but formality is likely to be difficult to overcome. Panels of three or more interviewers are very common in public-sector posts, such as teaching, and are usually held because various interest groups have a right to be there. Although bias may be reduced, there are real problems with establishing *rapport*. Panels may become more interested in each other's views than in those of the candidate, and require very careful chairing. Agreement beforehand about who will ask questions about which areas is crucial, otherwise one person may dominate the questioning.

Discrimination and equal opportunity legislation

It is obviously important that selection is done fairly. In addition to the social and legal obligations, there are increasing economic and demographic reasons for avoiding unfair bias. As recruitment becomes more difficult because of labour shortages, it makes economic sense to ensure that you are reaching every possible candidate.

The Equal Pay Act, 1970, was designed to stop discrimination in terms and conditions of employment between men and women. Equal pay for equal worth is how this is usually interpreted. The comparisons are made between people working for the same employer, at the same establishment.

The Sex Discrimination Act, 1975, aimed at removing discrimination in the non-contractual area of employment. A distinction is drawn between direct and indirect discrimination. An example of the latter would be advertising that applicants must be over six foot tall; most women would not be eligible. The Race Relations Act, 1976, and the Fair Employment (Northern Ireland) Act 1989 follow very similar lines.

The areas where discrimination most commonly occurs are in job advertisements, recruitment procedures, promotion, training and transfer policies. It is the responsibility of personnel departments to monitor these, and they should be able to help with specific problems. The Equal Opportunities Commission and the Commission for Racial Equality are specialist organizations for help in this area.

Implications for managers

Since all the points discussed in this and the following chapters are about implications for managers, this section will inevitably be shorter.

Finding and selecting staff is an exciting part of management—here is the opportunity to pick someone to make your section work better. It is worth spending some time thinking how most effectively to do so. As there is an increasing variety of people to select from, recruitment methods will have to be well thought out and targeted to ensure a suitable field of candidates.

Summary statements for managers

- Before recruitment starts managers should consider what changes need to be made in the job.
- Systematic recruitment means having a job description, a person specification and using recruitment methods which produce a suitable candidate at least cost.
- The more complex the job the more sophisticated a selection process may be appropriate.
- The selection interview is still the main method of selecting people.
- It is very important that recruitment and selection are fair.

References

1 ACAS have an excellent free booklet on the whole process of recruitment and selection: *Recruitment and selection*. Advisory Booklet No. 6, London, ACAS, 1986.
2 *Ibid.*, p. 4.
3 J. MUNROE FRASER, *Employment interviewing*. London, Macdonald &

Evans, 1950; A. RODGER, *The Seven-point Plan*. London, National Institute of Industrial Psychology, 1952.

4   For further detail see P. PLUMBLEY, *Recruitment and selection*, fifth edition. London, Institute of Personnel Management, 1991.

5   See, for example, R. F. WAGNER, 'The employment interview: a critical appraisal', *Personnel Psychology*, 2, 1949, pp. 17–40.

6   D. P. TORRINGTON, *Management Face to Face*. Hemel Hempstead, Prentice Hall, 1991.

10

Generating Competent Performers

This chapter examines some specific strategies for generating competent performance. Most of it is about training and development but there are also sections on coaching and mentoring. Often these strategies will be used by senior people in the organization to generate competence in those more junior. But not always: increasingly training is undertaken at the initiative of the individual who recognizes a need for self-development. Even appraisal may be initiated by the individual approaching the boss to ask, 'How am I getting on?'

Training and development

When we start a new job we usually feel very unsure, slightly scared and full of excitement. Our performance is erratic, awkward, enthusiastic and maybe long-winded. As time goes on most of us do things more smoothly and efficiently. In one sense we have become competent performers. Most of this is because we have developed whilst doing the job, but it is also due to the training we received, if only on the first day.

Training usually refers to specific activities geared to improving the skills and knowledge needed to achieve short-term objectives directly associated with the work to be done. An example would be training to use a new desk-top computer system. Development usually refers to less distinct objectives, to do with the longer term, difficult to define, objectives associated with personal improvement. An example would be a development programme for leadership.

Training and development, however integral to any work, can be resented by job holders if it is not felt to be appropriate. Managers may complain because they have to run their unit without the staff who are away training, and individuals can feel very demotivated if the training they receive seems a waste of time. It is also important to remember that not all problems can be solved by training. Some might be better solved by improved recruitment or investment in equipment. So what are the main purposes of training? Tyson and York list them as:

1 Maximising productivity and output.
2 Developing the versatility and employability of human resources.
3 Developing the cohesiveness of the whole organization and its sub-groups.
4 Increasing job satisfaction, motivation and morale.
5 Developing a consciousness of the importance of safety at work and improving standards.
6 Making the best use of available material, resources, equipment, and methods.
7 Standardizing organizational practices and procedures.[1]

Any or all of these may concern a particular department, manager or job holder. Line managers are responsible for, and will be involved in, identifying the training needs of their staff and in providing some of the learning experience. The training department, or personnel function, is responsible for co-ordinating the process across the organization, making the arrangements for training, designing courses, co-ordinating evaluation and being a source of expertise in training for line managers to consult.

Identification of training needs

A systematic approach to training and development starts with the identification of training needs. The argument is that this ensures that training and development are given because they are needed. To do this requires an evaluation of what the present and future work involves and what the present and future staff can do.

The identification of training needs also requires an understanding of organizational needs. For example, a general programme for all users when a new computer system is being introduced. It is also useful, but time consuming, to do an audit of the development of the organization. One of the most useful audit schemes is that used in schools. There has been a long tradition that managers in business have nothing to learn from those who manage in the public sector, whereas managers in the public sector have much to learn from business. This is rather shortsighted, as many managerial jobs in the public sector require a subtle and thoughtful approach. In addition some useful devices and techniques are being used in the public sector that could be borrowed with advantage. One of them is an approach to identifying training needs.

In schools a very common approach to this is doing a whole-school review, using a technique called GRIDS—a series of questions about the objectives and present position of the school.[2] The results may show that there is an over-competent staff who need no training but who deserve a lot of encouragement. On the other hand the review may show a deficiency. It might be met best with better equipment, reorganization or recruiting different staff. However, most often some training needs are identifiable. This process reveals training needs associated with the whole organization or department.

Individual training needs often arise from formal reports on performance such as appraisal, assessment centres or staff reports. These increasingly use lists of competencies which have been generated, either locally or nationally, to show what someone doing that job needs to be able to do. They may also include some form of self-assessment.

When performance has been assessed and areas of difficulty identified, an individual training or development plan can be drawn up. Here priorities are identified for the individual in relation to the other needs of the department or organization. Ideally these are then given target dates for training or development. This personal development plan may include formal training sessions, opportunities to go and find out what others are doing, experiences of various kinds, reading or video materials. The plans need to be monitored to ensure something results from all the time and effort put in by the individual and their manager to draw up the plan.

The reality for most organizations is that managers identify the training needs of their staff and departments far more informally. When asked how they identified training needs health authority managers in one district used such phrases as 'Talking to them,' 'Knowing their work,' and 'Seeing the way they handle things.'

Training techniques and methods

Chapter 3 contains a discussion of learning methods and examples of different ways of learning. What follows here is a brief guide to the more common methods of instruction, with their advantages and disadvantages. It is worth having another look at the models presented in chapter 3 and asking which of the methods are best suited to fulfilling each of the models.

Lecture. A talk given without much participation by the trainees. Suitable for large audiences, where the information to be got over can be worked out precisely in advance. There is little opportunity for feedback, so some may not get the point. Lectures require careful preparation and should not last longer than forty minutes.

Talk. A talk allowing participation by the trainees, by asking questions of them or questions being asked by them. Useful for getting over a new way of looking at things which requires some abstraction, for example some management idea or view of the future. It is suitable for giving information to up to twenty people. It works only where people are willing or able to participate. Where people do not want to participate it becomes a lecture.

Skill instruction. The trainee is told how to do it, shown how to do it, does it under supervision. This is suitable for putting across skills as long as the task is broken down into suitable parts. The breaking down into suitable parts will vary with the task and the person who is to receive the training. This form of training is not appropriate for all skills, as some tasks are best learnt as a whole.

On the job. Here trainees work in the real environment, with support from a skilled person. This gives the trainee real practice and it does not involve expensive new equipment. However, not all skilled people are skilled trainers.

Audio-visual presentation. This includes slides, films and video, which is by far the most common now. The technique is similar to a lecture in what it can achieve, but video has the additional advantage over a lecture that you can stop and start it as you want.

Programmed instruction. Trainees work at their own pace, using a book, computer program or interactive video which has a series of tasks and tests geared to teaching something systematically. It is suitable for learning logical skills and knowledge. It does not allow discussion with others. This may be important, in which case the application may be debatable.

Discussion. Knowledge, ideas and opinions are exchanged between trainees and trainer. This is particularly suitable, where the application is a matter of opinion, for changing attitudes and finding out how knowledge is going to be applied. The technique requires skill on the part of the trainer, as it can be difficult to keep discussion focused and useful.

Role-playing. Trainees are asked to act out the role they, or someone else, would play at work. It is used particularly for face-to-face situations. It is suitable for nearly real-life work, where criticism would be useful. The difficulties are that trainees can be embarrassed and the usefulness is very dependent on the quality of the feedback.

Case study. A history of some event is outlined and the trainees are invited to analyse the causes of a problem or find a solution. This provides an opportunity for a cool look at problems and for the exchange of ideas about possible solutions. However, trainees may not realize that the real world is not quite the same as the training session.

Exercise. Trainees perform a particular task, in a particular way, to get a particular result. This is suitable when trainees need practice in following a procedure or formula to reach a required objective. The exercise must be realistic.

Project. Similar to an exercise but with greater freedom to display initiative and creative ideas. Projects provide feedback on a range of personal qualities. They need the full interest and co-operation of the trainee.

Group dynamics. Trainees are put into a situation where the behaviour of the individuals and the group is examined. The task usually requires the group to co-operate before they can achieve the objective. Observers collect information about how the trainees go about it and there is feedback to the group and to individuals when the task is completed. Trainees learn about the effect they have on others. It may be threatening, and anxieties need to be resolved before the end of the session. Again this depends heavily on the quality of the trainer and can be dangerous if entered on too casually.

Management development

The training and development of managers has been a fascinating subject throughout this century. Analysis of what it is that managers do has been the subject of many books. Some are biographies.[3] Some are systematic studies of what managers do.[4] There has never been one model that everyone agrees on. The reason is partly that managerial jobs differ, partly that we do not really know what managing is, partly that managing is an abstract activity which is difficult to measure, and partly that people hold differing political and moral views about what managing should be.

The current approach to management training and development is to develop lists of competences which managers need if they are to be effective, and then train or develop them. The current interest in competences was developed by R. E. Boyatzis,[5] and the term includes not only skills but also mind sets and personal attributes. The lists are usually generated by committees of experienced trainers and practitioners debating what should be included. Figure 21 shows a list generated by the Management Charter Initiative in 1991. Each of the sections is broken down into its component parts. There are currently two levels for MCI aimed at junior and middle managers, a level three aimed at senior managers is planned. Although MCI standards are not universal there are similar models being developed in many organizations and professional bodies.

The training and development of managers which takes place can be of all sorts. Some will comprise formal courses which include lectures, videos, exercises and group discussion. Some will involve on-the-job coaching and mentoring. Some will be experimental learning, such as outdoor activities to develop team work and leadership. There is constant development of ideas and not infrequent changes in fashion in management training and development. Careful evaluation of methods is difficult when the work of managing is so ill defined. The competence movement is an attempt to overcome this.

Figure 21
Occupational Standards for Managers
(Management I)

Key Purpose: To Achieve the Organisation's Objectives and Continuously Improve its Performance

Key Roles and their associated Units of Competence

Key Role Manage Operations

I 1　Maintain and improve service and product operations

I 2　Contribute to the implementation of change in services, products and systems

Key Role Manage Finance

I 3　Recommend, monitor and control the use of resources

I 4　Contribute to the recruitment and selection of personnel

I 5　Develop teams, individuals and self to enhance performance

Key Role Manage People

I 6　Plan, allocate and evaluate work carried out by teams, individuals and self

I 7　Create, maintain and enhance effective working relationships

Key Role Manage Information

I 8　Seek, evaluate and organise information for action

I 9　Exchange information to solve problems and make decisions

Source: *MCI 1991*

Occupational Standards for Managers
(Management II)

Key Purpose: *To Achieve the Organisation's Objectives and Continuously Improve its Performance*	

Key Roles and their associated Units of Competence

Key Role Manage Operations

> II 1 Initiate and implement change and improvement in services, products and systems

> II 2 Monitor, maintain and improve service and product delivery

Key Role Manage Finance

> II 3 Monitor and control the use of resources

> II 4 Secure effective resource allocation for activities and projects

Key Role Manage People

> II 5 Recruit and select personnel

> II 6 Develop teams, individuals and self to enhance performance

> II 7 Plan, allocate and evaluate work carried out by teams, individuals and self

> II 8 Create, maintain and enhance effective working relationships

Key Role Manage Information

> II 9 Seek, evaluate and organise information for action

> II 10 Exchange information to solve problems and make decisions

Figure 21 *contd*

Coaching and mentoring

Coaching is improving the performance of someone who is already competent; it is not suitable for initial training. It is usually done on a one-to-one basis, set in the everyday working environment, and is a continuing activity. It is gently nudging people to improve their performance, develop their skills and increase their confidence. It is helping people to take on more responsibility and develop their career prospects. Although it is usually done by people with their immediate subordinates, this is not essential. Many's the time a new boss has been coached by an established team. The main prerequisites are expertise, experience and judgement. The essence of coaching is delegation and discussion.

Delegation is not giving people jobs to do; it is giving people scope, responsibility and authority. The questions to ask are: can the person test their own ideas, develop understanding and confidence? The more specific the instructions and terms of reference, the less learning will be possible as a result of the activity. When the assignment is delegated the person being coached starts to work but also takes the initiative in seeking guidance and discussion with the coach. Too much help, and the person leans on the coach; too little and he may lose confidence. This is where the coach needs to exercise judgement.

Discussion depends on a good working relationship where comments are welcomed, not resented or mistrusted. The coach can help analyse problems and generate alternative choices. Criticism and praise need to be specific, and geared to facts and behaviour rather than opinions.

Using the sequence suggested by Kolb's learning cycle (see chapter 3) can be a useful way to structure coaching experience. The coach's role would be to move the person being coached on to the next step in the cycle by asking appropriate questions. If, for example, I were coaching you on how to run meetings, we might start by asking you to chair a small meeting. This is the concrete experience. You then reflect on your own performance— how did you ensure you finished on time, how did you make sure everyone got a turn, etc? We then discuss how the answers can be generalized to other meetings. Do you need to be forceful about keeping to the agenda? Do you need to decide in advance which are the items to be discussed longest? And so on. You then have another go trying a new method.

Specific examples of coaching are shadowing people at work, hand-over time, job exchanges and mentoring. The last has become very popular for management development. It involves someone senior in the organization taking particular responsibility for a junior manager, discussing their work with them and ensuring that they get a variety of opportunities. One set of advice for mentors is:

* Manage the relationship.
* Encourage the protégé.
* Nurture the protégé.
* Teach the protégé.
* Offer mutual respect.
* Respond to the protégé's needs.

Evaluation and validation of training

If work organizations are to spend resources on training it is important to evaluate whether the training really proves useful. Validation is the word used to describe the process of seeing whether the training has achieved its objectives. Evaluation is the process of ascertaining whether the training has affected the performance of the job. It may be that an Outward Bound course on leadership meets all the course objectives, the validation, but we cannot see any change in performance at work, the evaluation. Evaluation is much more difficult because of the problems of deciding, defining and measuring performance. This is particularly difficult with abstract performance such as management.

Hamblin suggests five levels on which evaluation may take place:[6]

* *Reaction.* The training is subjectively evaluated by the trainees on completion. They give their personal views and impressions of the value of the training.
* *Learning.* Measuring the amount of learning that has taken place in the training, reliably and validly. This is what is called validation.
* *Job behaviour.* Assessing how much of the training has affected the work performance about six to nine months later.
* *Organization.* The impact of training on the whole organization

is measured, using criteria such as productivity, time taken to do work, waste material, absenteeism, labour turnover, running costs.

• *Ultimate level.* Trying to assess the effect of training on profitability and growth. For example, some of the training in customer care in the service industry in the 1980s may account for increased profitability in that sector since.

Implications for management

Generating competent performers is perhaps the most important task of management. It is this that will ensure the survival of the business. It is done in all sorts of ways. It is the responsibility of management to organize the materials and work into suitable chunks, so that properly selected and trained people willingly perform well.

Summary statements for managers

• Generating competent performance is what management is about.
• Identifying training needs should include those of the individual and those of the organization.
• There are many different techniques for training. The ideal is to select the appropriate one for the type of learning taking place.
• Coaching and mentoring are both part of managing of people.
• Evaluating training is difficult but very useful for a systematic approach.

References

1 S. TYSON and A. YORK, *Personnel management made simple*. London, Heinemann, 1982, p. 178.
2 See A MCMAHON, R. BOLEM and P. HOLLY, *Guidelines for review and internal development in schools: primary/secondary school handbook GRIDS*. Schools Council Programme No. 1, York, Longman and Schools Council, 1984.
3 Such as J. HARVEY-JONES, *Making it happen*. London, Collins, 1988.

4 For example, John Kotter's very readable study of *The general managers*. New York, Free Press, 1982.

5 R. E. BOYATZIS, *The competent manager: a model for effective performance*. Chichester, Wiley, 1982.

6 A. HAMBLIN, *Evaluation and control of training*. London, McGraw-Hill, 1974.

11

Performance Management

This book, and the accompanying books in the series, are all in some sense about generating competent performance. The whole business of management is about generating sufficiently competent performance so that the organization can deliver a service or product. It is very difficult to start defining the job required of an individual without a description of what the organization is in existence for, and what the financial targets and constraints are. Once we know those we can start defining the various jobs that need doing. When we know what job is required we can decide how well we want it done, and so reach a basis for judging competent performance. This will include an understanding, explicit or implicit, of what would be the consequences of the job being done less well and what the benefits of it being done better. Obviously, jobs vary in what is meant by competent performance. Until we have described the job we cannot recruit systematically, nor can we allocate specific work to individuals. Agreeing what it is we are trying to do, and the standard we are aiming for, is the beginning of what we mean by competent performance. This whole book is focused on understanding individuals, so that we can appreciate what it is reasonable to expect from any particular person. It is anticipated that competent performance is more likely to be generated if we communicate successfully with each other, work in groups better, and develop our credibility as managers.

Ensuring competent performance requires an examination of various aspects of the work context.

Job characteristics

Most jobs develop over quite a long period of time. They develop in different ways. First, there is the general development, such as bus driving, that comes into existence in different places—driving different types of buses, on different routes. Second, the job

Figure 22

Job dimensions and their effects

1. *Skill variety*. The way a job demands a variety of different activities that involve using a number of different skills and talents.	
2. *Task identity*. The way a job requires the job holder to complete a whole and coherent piece of work having a tangible outcome.	These give meaning to the work people do.
3. *Task significance*. The way a job has an impact on the lives or work of other people, inside the organization or outside.	
4. *Autonomy*. The way a job holder enjoys freedom from supervision, independence and discretion in deciding how the job should be done.	This gives responsibility to job holders.
5. *Feedback*. The way the job holder receives clear and direct information about their effectiveness.	This gives the job holder knowledge of results.

Source: Based on J. R. Hackman, 'Work design', in *Motivation and work behaviour*, ed. R. M. Steers *and* L. W. Porter, London, McGraw-Hill, 1989.

develops specifically for the particular organization, as driving the local mini-bus is a different job from driving a continental tour bus. Third, the job develops with the particular job holder, such as one bus driver being chatty, another helpful to old folk and mothers with prams. Differences between similar jobs affect recruitment, training, payment and effectiveness. Seldom would the same people apply for the two bus driving jobs mentioned. Some people will be more motivated by one job than by the other, and vice versa.

J. R. Hackman suggests there are various dimensions in jobs, associated with good performance by the job holder.[3] (See figure 22.) These dimensions give meaning to work, responsibility to the job holder and knowledge of how he is doing. By taking various actions (see figure 23) managers can get good results on these job dimensions and so improve the motivation and performance of job holders. Terms commonly used to describe this process are job design, job enlargement and job enrichment.

Job design or, more commonly, job redesign, is the process of getting the optimum fit between the organizational requirements of the individual employee and the individual's need for satisfaction in doing the job. In the past managers have concentrated on designing jobs so simply that anyone can do them and all that was required was suitable rewards and supervision, the carrot-and-stick method. The last few decades have seen managers concentrate more on trying to find jobs that are whole. Research suggests that this wholeness motivates people more than the carrot and stick. There are two well known approaches to job redesign: job enlargement and job enrichment.

Job enlargement extends the scope of jobs by combining two or more jobs into one, or by taking a number of work functions and putting them together in a single job with a greater variety and wholeness. The expansion is horizontal. An example is Marks & Spencer salespeople, who not only take our money at the cash desk but also stock the racks and redistribute the 'returns'; they have a whole area, such as lingerie, to look after.

Job enrichment is a method that gives people more responsibility for setting their own pace, deciding their own methods and putting right their own mistakes, so increasing their autonomy. The expansion is vertical. An example is the primary nursing system in hospital, where each qualified nurse has their own patients, or a small ward, to look after rather than sharing them, with one senior nurse taking the important decisions and allocating the work.

The immediate work environment

Chapter 6 dealt with the material on working in groups and the effect they have on us. Most of us are motivated by belonging to a group of people whom we value and who make us feel we belong. As discussed in chapter 8, most of us are also motivated to work better if our supervisor, or boss, has credibility. Several specific management initiatives have been used in the last few years to nurture these aspects of teamwork and leadership.

Team briefing, where the top manager tells their immediate subordinates important information or ideas. The subordinates in turn tell their immediate subordinates. The process repeats itself

Figure 23
Ways of getting good results on the five job dimensions

Action	Job dimension affected
1. *Forming natural work units* so that the work to be done has a logic and makes sense to the job holder.	2, 3
2. *Combining tasks* so that a number of natural work units may be put together to make a bigger and more coherent job.	1, 2
3. *Establishing links with clients* so that the job holder has contact with the people using the service or product the job holder is supplying.	1, 4, 5
4. *Vertical loading* so that job holders take on more of the management of their jobs in deciding what to do, organizing their own time, solving their own problems and controlling their own costs.	4
5. *Opening feedback channels* so that job holders can discover more about how they are doing and whether their performance is improving or deteriorating.	5

Source: Based on J. R. Hackman, 'Work design' *op cit.*

until everyone in the organization (or that part of it, in a very large organization) has been given the information. The idea is that everyone gets to hear the same information, rapidly and face-to-face, so there are opportunities for clarification. It is not always clear how much information can go the other way—up the team briefing system.

Team building. Various strategies have been used here. One is taking everyone for a week or a weekend to a comfortable hotel to pursue some systematic group exercises led by a trainer. Sometimes the time may be spent on purely social activities. Another way is having a specific task that everyone in the group needs to become involved in. For example, in one hospital each department was asked to do a Quality Assurance review in which it had to identify the department, the staff, the service it provided, what the quality issues were and plans for the future. The top management suggested it was done in groups.

Quality circles. This is where small departmental groups of five to ten volunteers meet regularly, primarily in order to resolve quality-related problems. They look not at large-scale problems so much as at those niggling local issues which are within members' scope to resolve but of which management may not be aware. Members need to be trained in data collection, presentation and meeting skills. They may use brainstorming techniques to generate ideas. An example would be reducing some of the paperwork in the accounts department by one person filing in two sections. Another would be moving a machine on the shop floor to improve the flow of work.

Leadership. The Industrial Society, amongst others, runs a number of courses on leadership. Most of them emphasize the need for individual managers to be able to motivate their staff. Motivation and leadership can become something of a tautology, but undoubtedly the two ideas are related in management-oriented training and thinking. Openness, trust, credibility, allowing participation, getting things done, spelling out the mission, are all part of leadership and motivation. Chapter 8 has some ideas about this area.[4]

The immediate work environment can be very demoralizing if the group and leader are not to one's liking. A team leader or department manager needs to think carefully how each member is finding the work of the group as a whole. The manager needs to ask questions such as: Is someone being left out who does not want to be? Can everyone who wants a say voice their opinion? Who is the odd one out? Do they mind?

The contract idea

Motivating people at work is very much a management idea. It is something managers must do to employees to get the best out of them. Sophisticated human resource management experts would never put it as crudely, but essentially that is the point. One way of looking at the balance is to think in terms of contracts. Enid

Mumford introduced this idea, which was taken up by Torrington and Chapman.[5]

The argument is that members of an organization are employed to work, and they take up employment in order to work. The basic contract is for work. A feature of the contract is mutual control, with the degree and nature of the control varying. A traditional view is that managers tell others what to do and then monitor their performance to make sure it has been done properly. At the same time individuals seek to control the demands the organization makes on them. These moves towards mutual control have a core of informal understanding rather than overt agreement. In addition there are collective contracts such as the terms and conditions of employment. The control of managers, representing the organization, and the control of employees, individuals, are balanced by various contracts. Some are informal, such as the culture that develops in a company. Think of the joking way many people may control their boss. Some of the contracts are formal, for example job descriptions and rule books.

The idea of contracts is a useful one for managers in thinking of the relative rights and obligations of the employee and the employer as represented by the manager. Questions of fairness, reasonableness and trust are associated with the whole business of motivating others. Using the phrase 'motivating people at work' suggests that coercive power is not going to be used to ensure compliance. But some sort of framework is helpful to distinguish the highly manipulative managerial strategy from the 'felt fair' strategy. The contract model, although not new, is a simple device for keeping track of these different rights whilst under the pressure of making things happen.

Monitoring performance

How do we know how well things are going? How do we know if an individual is performing well? The two extremes are usually easy to discriminate and need no sophisticated management techniques to reveal them. But, for the vast majority of employees who fall between the two, it may be rather more difficult to judge how well they are performing. Are there any particular techniques for doing so?

Monitoring various indicators that may suggest there is a problem is useful to managers of large departments. These give early warning of matters that are hindering employee effectiveness. Monitoring needs to be carefully considered, as too much monitoring of the wrong things can be demotivating on its own. No one likes to feel they are under close surveillance. Monitoring outcomes is always better than monitoring behaviour. Some commonly used monitoring devices are given below.

Productivity. Various statistics can be worked out: output or throughput per person per hour, added value per total number of employees, proportion of productive time over total available time, percentage capacity utilization, percentage of idle time, percentage labour costs over total costs. Many of these are more suited to manufacturing industries but service industries can also use some of them. The comparison between this year and last, this month and last, similar departments or individuals, will reveal unusual productivity and consequently a possible performance problem.

Quality. Many industries now have Quality Assurance certification, often BSI 5750. Here procedures are laid down for doing the job, and others in the organization, as well as customers, can raise incidents where quality is seen to be inadequate. Monitoring the frequency of such incidents may show a person or section who are having problems.

Absence. Out of a normal 250 working days per year employees are likely to be absent between 10 and 30 per cent of the time. Some of this will be annual leave and or training; some will be for sickness. Working out weekly, monthly or yearly absence rates for individuals, groups and departments can indicate which are experiencing higher-than-average absence rates, which may indicate a problem of motivation. (See figure 24.)

Turnover. Similarly turnover of staff leaving can be worked out for sections, units or departments. It can be compared with others' or with last year's figures. There are also figures for comparison in the Department of Employment *Gazette*, which provides information for different regions and industries. Where the figure is higher than normal, questions about management might be appropriately asked. (See figure 24.)

Clearly, quantity is not everything and different industries will have different figures for what is usual. But if someone, or some department, differs in its performance from last year, or by comparison with others, there are inevitably questions to be asked. Enquiries could be made about the job, how it is organized, the

Figure 24
Measuring absence and turnover

Measuring absence, 1. Lost time

This shows the percentage of working time that has been lost through employee absence over a given period of time:

$$\frac{\text{Number of days lost through absence}}{\text{Average number of employees} \times \text{number of days}} \times 100$$

Example. In a workforce of eighty, two people are absent for one whole day each and ten are absent for half a day each, over a period of five days:

$$\frac{7}{80 \times 5} \ 100 = 1.75\%$$

Measuring absence, 2. Frequency

This shows the extent of the absence across the workforce by showing the number of times people are absent. This can be a useful refinement, as frequent short absences can be a bigger problem than rarer long spells.

$$\frac{\text{Number of absences}}{\text{Average number of employees}} \times 100$$

Example. Using the same figures as in the first example:

$$\frac{12}{80} \times 100 = 15\%$$

Measuring turnover, 1. Separation

The number of people leaving the organization or department is shown as a percentage of the total establishment:

$$\frac{\text{Number of leavers}}{\text{Number of employees}} \times 100$$

Example. Over a period, eighty-five people leave from a workforce of 300.

$$\frac{85}{300} \times 100 = 28.3\%$$

Measuring turnover, 2. Stability

As many of those who leave organizations do so in the early weeks of employment, it can be useful to measure the underlying stability by using the formula

$$\frac{\text{Number of employees with more than 12 months' service}}{\text{Average number of employees}} \times 100$$

Source: D. Torrington *and* J. Weightman, *Action Management,* London, Institute of Personnel Management, 1991.

'climate' in the group, the management, the reward system, and so on.

Individual performance appraisal

Appraising performance involves judgement and reporting. Both can be unreliable and subjective. Despite these problems the potential advantages of performance appraisal are so great that the effort is worth expending to make it work. The reasons why seniors may wish to appraise juniors in the organization include:

Human resource considerations. To ensure that the ability and energies of individuals are being used effectively. Through performance appraisal they hope to find out more about those who work for them and consequently make better use of each individual's talents and experience.

Training. Identifying training needs so the contribution of individuals may be developed. This may mean planning training for new tasks in the coming year or devising training to remedy poor performance.

Promotion. Appraisal can assist decision-making. Talking to the individual about their aspirations as well as finding out about their performance will help the decisions about promotion. Not everyone is seeking promotion.

Planning. To identify skill shortages and succession needs. Performance appraisal may demonstrate a widespread lack of suitable skills in the organization that needs some thought. This may require training or redeployment. It may be that some planned development needs to be delayed whilst it takes place.

Authority. Appraisal sustains the hierarchy of authority by confirming the dependence of subordinates on those who carry out the appraisals. It is one of the rituals that underlines who is the boss.

The reasons why juniors may wish to be appraised by their seniors include:

Performance. Ability to do the job can be enhanced by an emphasis on strengths and an understanding of what changes are needed. Here is an opportunity to discuss what could be done and how one might go about doing it.

Motivation. Reassurance can increase the level of enthusiasm and commitment. Talking about the job and the work it involves may remind us of why we do the job and why we wanted it in the first place.

Career. Individuals can obtain guidance and indicators about possible job changes. A boss may know of jobs going elsewhere in the organization and what experience and training are relevant. They often understand the promotion and careers prospects well, as they have travelled the same route themselves.

There are several reasons for having a formal system of appraisal:

* It provides the opportunity for a concerted effort to train all managers to improve and standardize practices.
* There is time to take stock and evaluate achievements and objectives.
* Many managers are not as well informed about their subordinates and their feelings as they think.
* Managers gain information about the way the department is working generally.
* There are lots of bad managers who, left to their own devices, would do little about constructive appraisal of performance.

Many things can impair the judgement and reporting of those doing performance appraisal. For example:

* Prejudice.
* Insufficient knowledge of the appraisee.
* The 'halo effect' of general likability or of recent events.
* The difficulty of distinguishing appraisees from the context in which they work.
* Different perceptions of what standards are appropriate.

Other problems associated with performance appraisal are:

The paperwork required, which is aimed at consistent reporting. In most organizations the paperwork is reinvented every three years, with a new form and forced choices about which boxes need filling in. There appears to be no solution to this one. However, despite the problems of the paperwork, it is worth remembering that the performance_appraisal interview is perhaps the most important part, and should be the focus—not the paperwork, which is often felt as an irritation.

The formality which the interview requires to distinguish it from a chat. Where a boss and subordinate work closely together, having a formal interview feels rather peculiar. It is worth setting aside a time and place for the process, as there are probably things you have not told each other in detail during the last year that are worth exploring. This is particularly so when there is a good, close team working together: individual differences often get sublimated in the interests of the group.

The 'just above average' syndrome. On a five-point scale people mark each other just above average. To be rated average is seen in some way as poor. Some organizations force appraisers to use at least two scores below average on their form. This develops into an informal understanding that being below average on a particular two scales is all right.

Ignoring the outcome. If the performance appraisal leads to no improved resources, training, career moves or changes in practice there is not much incentive for people to get involved next time round. One good reason for involving the boss in performance appraisal, rather than colleagues, who might understand the specifics of the performance better, is that the boss can often influence the use of resources.

The problem-solving approach is considered the most effective if both appraiser and appraisee have the skill and ability to handle the situation. This is similar to counselling (see chapter 13), where neither party knows the answer before the interview begins. It develops as the interaction takes place. Training in this type of interviewing is widely available.

Performance appraisal in various guises is now very common. Different forms are constantly being introduced to try to resolve some of the difficulties listed above. Despite the problems most people feel that a regular, formal encounter between themselves and their boss is an appropriate, if sometimes disappointing, procedure.

Implications for management

This chapter has been about specific ways of looking at the performance of those who work for you. The final chapter of this book is about what to do if this goes wrong.

Performance management emphasises the results of people's behaviour. However, the sequence input-process-output-outcome is worth checking as problems with results may arise from any point in the sequence.

Summary statements for managers

* Managers can redesign jobs to increase motivation.
* Various strategies are available for nurturing teams and leadership.
* Managers can use a variety of monitoring devices to indicate a potential problem with performance.
* The idea of an implicit, as well as explicit, contract between the employee and the employing organization is useful in keeping a balance when considering motivating people at work.

References

1 J. R. HACKMAN, 'Work design', in *Motivation and work behaviour*, ed. R. M. Steers and L. W. Porter. London, McGraw-Hill, 1987, pp. 467–93.
2 See also the books in this series by D. FARNHAM, *The corporate environment*, and M. ARMSTRONG, *Management processes and functions*, London, Institute of Personnel Management, 1990.
3 E. MUMFORD, 'Job satisfaction: a method of analysis', *Personnel Review*, summer 1972; D. P. TORRINGTON and J. CHAPMAN, *Personnel management*. Hemel Hempstead, Prentice Hall, 1979.

12

Reward Systems

Growing attention is paid by managements to the culture of the organizations they run. This is based on the belief that the norms and values that a working group hold in common are more influential on their collective performance than is the way they are organized. Pay arrangements are central to cultural initiatives as they are the most tangible expression of the working relationship between employer and employee.

Reward systems usually mean the financial rewards an organization gives its employees in return for their labour. These used to be called the renumeration package but employers and their personnel departments have become increasingly interested in using pay systems to influence the performance of individuals by rewarding particular aspects, and so they are now often called reward systems.

Employees' views

Employees are usually interested in at least the following aspects of their pay package.

Purchasing power, the absolute level of earnings. Without motivating greatly in itself, it can be very *de*motivating if it is too low. For example, if the retail price index has gone up by 10 per cent but pay has only gone up 5 per cent anyone will feel hard done by.

Felt fair. Every employee has strong feelings about whether the level of pay is fair for the job. We all seem to have a 'felt fair' scale in our mind by which we measure each job. Some seem exploitative, others generous, and so on in between. If Herzberg (see chapter 4) is right the exploitative is likely to be demotivating rather than the generous being motivating.

Rights. These concern the relative distribution of wealth within the organization. When companies are doing well and directors are receiving large pay rises as well as a distribution of shares, employees feel the system is unreasonable and that they have a right to a larger share of the profits.

Relativities. Am I getting a fair deal in relation to others? For example, teachers compare themselves with graduates in nursing and the police force. Sometimes they feel relatively well paid, at others less so. When they compare themselves with graduates in the financial world they usually feel relatively poorly paid. No doubt this led to some of the low morale of teachers at the end of the 1980s. However, high morale is not just about high relative pay.

Composition: how the pay is made up. Is there overtime, a pension, a company car, etc? Individuals vary considerably in the particular composition that suits them. As we saw in chapter 5, we all have different orientations to work, so will look for different packages. Employers are trying to make use of this by negotiating individual pay packages. This can be motivating unless people feel that others are being offered, or are negotiating, better packages for themselves. Trade unions will see a place for themselves in helping individuals to negotiate a better deal in line with their colleagues.

Employers' views

The *employer*, or the personnel department, is likely to think about the following when devising a pay package.

Competition. This is where considerations come into play of how much needs to be paid to attract, and keep, suitable employees. What are others in the field, in the same locality, rewarding their staff with?

Control. Employers use pay to deal with the fluctuations in work, for example, overtime, part-time work, contract work, piece-work. No employer wants to pay full-time, permanent staff when they are only needed occasionally. Hence the use of peripheral staff.

Productivity. Incentive schemes are reinvented frequently to encourage productivity. They have a built-in bias towards quantity rather than quality, as the latter is always more difficult to measure. Performance-related pay is the current phrase to describe this.

Cost. What is the true cost of employing people? It includes not only their pay but such things as their recruitment, training and pensions.

Careers. Do we want a reward system which encourages people to stay—for example, increments and pensions? Or do we want people to do specific jobs and then leave—immediate performance-related pay? The core/periphery groups of staff are very much related to this discussion, with most organizations going for a bit of both.

These two groups of thoughts about payment (employees' and employers') do not easily go together. It is not surprising, then, that payment schemes are constantly being rearranged as the various parties try another possible resolution of their different orientations. Perhaps reward systems and their administration are the most graphic example of the plurality of organizations.

Current practices in rewards at work tend to emphasize the individual at the expense of the collective. This is likely to lead to problems over relativities in the future, but at the moment it is felt that individually negotiated pay will motivate, and keep, the high performers. Some sort of *performance-related pay* has been introduced to most management groups.

Another force for change towards individually negotiated reward systems is the difficulty of recruiting particular types of employee, for example experienced systems engineers in the computing world. Similar is the difficulty of recruiting in particular parts of the country, for example nurses and teachers in parts of London and the Home Counties. There are pressures to move away from the nationally agreed pay negotiations that have been commonplace in the public sector particularly for the last sixty years. Managers are likely to be in favour of individual contracts for their subordinates, as it gives more autonomy and greater control over both their unit and their subordinates.

Performance-related pay

There has been much discussion by management experts[1] in the past ten years about performance management. Managers inevitably influence performance and they often hope to improve it. Frequently organizations have sought to achieve this by introducing appraisal systems and performance-related pay (PRP).

These both emphasize individual performance. For many employees and their organizations, this has meant an enormous cultural change when there has previously been a tradition of collective bargaining or traditional incentive schemes.
A typical systematic PRP sequence would be:

1 A grade for the job is derived using job evaluation techniques.
2 A development plan for each individual is devised.
3 Individual performance is evaluated using a series of headings such as:
 –Team working
 –Decision-making
 –Initiative
 –Creativity
 –Safety
 –Planning.
4 A ranking is given to each individual out of the following: unacceptable/acceptable/good/very good/excellent/exceptional.
5 These are then compared with a matrix so that those with a higher ranking get a larger pay rise than those below.

The claims made for introducing PRP are:[2]

• Improvements in staff levels of commitment.
• Easier identification of training needs.
• Improved job satisfaction.
• Opportunity to harmonize conditions.
• Improved communication between supervisor and subordinates.

The difficulties associated with PRP are:

• Carrying out the appraisals.
• Individuals concentrating on objectives related to pay rather than to their whole job.
• Translating appraisals into pay.
• Trade union attitudes.
• The cost of running the system.
• The demotivating effect on those ranked average.
• Perceived unfairness, e.g. the highest paid are getting more at the expense of the lower paid.

- The lack of evaluation of the effectiveness of PRP.
- The effect on team culture.

Integration and harmonization of pay and conditions

In many organizations, the rewards system includes both differences of pay and differences of holidays, sick pay, pensions, company cars, hours and other benefits and allowances. Often this has led to an extraordinary number of different levels, for example in one region of the National Health Service, in 1990, they were paying 87,000 people on 2,008 different rates of pay each with associated terms and conditions.

This creates several problems. A large amount of administration is necessary to ensure that everyone gets what they are entitled to. The opportunity is there for anyone looking for regrading to find an anomaly or comparator to justify their case. Such an inflexible and unco-ordinated system makes the implementation of other aspects of pay policy, such as PRP, more complicated than it needs to be.

With a common pay structure, an integrated pay scheme, and harmonization of conditions, the only difference between grades is due to responsibility. This is called a single-status arrangement. There are several advantages to this. First, equal pay for equal value legislation points to the logic of single-status systems. Second, there is now greater emphasis on seeking the involvement and commitment of all employees, against which differences in status may stand as an obstacle. Third, the current belief in the development of the human resource means that organizations need to try and integrate all their staff.

Non-pay rewards

So far this chapter has only dealt with financial rewards at work. There are, of course, other rewards that can be used. The theories of motivation outlined in chapter 4 have been used by management experts to devise non-pay rewards for people at work. If we refer to Herzberg's theory of motivation and Steers and Porter's comparison of 'general patterns of managerial approaches to motivation' (figures 7 and 8) we can see that each of these models might choose to use different non-pay rewards. The traditional model would reward people by ensuring that the supervision was appropriate; the human relations model would reward individuals with attention and keeping them informed; the human resource model would reward individuals by allowing them to use their potential for creativity and control.

However tempting it is for managers, human resource experts and personnel departments to assume that the latest rewards system will be effective, the material described in chapter 5 about different orientations to work should be a warning not to treat everyone the same. It may well be true that some people work for attention and others for self-fulfilment and control of their own time, but many others prefer to keep a simple instrumental approach to work and get their other satisfactions elsewhere. This does not necessarily mean they are less committed employees – they are just looking for different rewards compared to the current orthodoxy of everyone looking for fulfilment at work.

Implications for managers

Reward systems are usually set at an organization-wide level, even where there is decentralized bargaining. These reward systems may try to reward individual performance or be aimed at collective effort. Any individual manager is unlikely to have much control over the reward systems, particularly payment systems. There are, however, the other less tangible rewards, such as job allocation, monitoring and communication, which can be used by individual managers. The material described in the next chapter may help in thinking about some of these.

Summary statements for managers

- Pay is a manifestation of the relationship between employers and employees.
- Employers and employees do not necessarily have compatable views about the best way of paying people.
- Current practice is to move away from collective pay schemes towards individual, performance-related schemes.
- Single-status arrangements, where everyone has the same terms

and conditions and are on the same pay structure, are increasingly favoured by employers and employees.
• Pay is not the only reason why individuals work. There are other rewards that motivate us to give our effort to our employer.

References

1   F. NEALE (ed.) *The Handbook of Performance Management.* London, IPM, 1991
2   N. KINNIE and D. LOWE 'Performance Related Pay on the Shopfloor.' *Personnel Management,* November 1990.

13

Dealing with Problem People

There are all sorts of problem people. For example, there are those who are unhappy, those who make others unhappy and those who are unable to fit in. Most of their problems have nothing to do with employing organizations and are not the subject of this book. However, we are concerned here with those who are a problem in the work environment. At some point we have all worked with people whose work is not satisfactory. We have all worked too with people who are a problem because they distract others from doing satisfactory work. Usually both problems are temporary and we are tolerant of the disruption. An example of someone who temporarily is a poor worker might be the travel agent whose computer is 'down', so that he or she is unable to discover whether there are vacancies on the holiday the client wants. An example of the second might be the colleague celebrating a forthcoming marriage and going round chatting to everyone.

In most employing organizations it is the responsibility of management to ensure that the work is distributed in suitable chunks, with appropriate materials and resources, to suitably selected and trained people. But even the best-run section, department or organization will have problems sometimes. There may be a problem with the materials, the organization of the work, the selection and training of staff or some idiosyncratic problem. Most such cases are short-lived and cause only minor irritations. Indeed, it can be argued that one of the main tasks of middle managers is to deal with these differences between plan and reality.

Problems with people at work can be short-term or long-term. For example, most people tend not to function very well when they have a cold. But there are others who never seem to perform well. There can also be groups of people who are a problem as well as individuals. For example, a group who have set group norms (see chapter 6) that are not compatible with those of the rest of the department or organization. This chapter is mostly concerned with the individual who has a long-term problem with performance at work. It summarizes the possible reasons for poor performance, drawing together material that has been discussed in more detail in earlier chapters.

Establishing the gap

Before anything can be done to improve poor performance it is important to establish that there really *is* a gap between required and actual performance.

Required performance is communicated to individuals in several ways. Everyone is supposed to have a contract of employment that outlines basic duties and conditions of work. In addition most organizations have formal rule books, job descriptions, training manuals, standards and procedures. Expectations are also communicated informally through briefing meetings, training sessions, meetings and individually. There may be reasons for an individual's difficulties in any of these. For example, the descriptions, procedures and standards may be poorly thought out, inappropriate or out of date. Even if the prescriptions are paragons of perfection they are useless if they are poorly communicated. See chapter 7 for discussion of problems with communication, for example the importance of the frame of reference.

Information about actual performance can be collected in several ways. First, there are records, such as personal files, time sheets, sickness and absence records, work and record cards. Second, there are other people who come into contact with the individual, such as colleagues; customers' complaints; other departments who may be a source of information. A third source is making a comparison with other people who do similar work, e.g. in the amount of unfinished work, wastage or complaints.

After looking at what is expected and what has actually been done the question is whether there is a sufficient gap between the two to require attention.

Reasons for problem performance

Only by finding the reason, or reasons, for the gap between expected and actual performance can we begin to do something about it. There are three main types of reason for poor performance. First are personal reasons that arise from the person's domestic and individual circumstances. Second are the reasons to do with poor management or organization. The third type is personal reasons that arise from the individual not fitting in with the organization.[1]

Personal characteristics

Personal characteristics, outside the organization's control, that might impede performance fall into several categories. They produce the ethical dilemma of how long and to what extent the organization should allow personal problems to interfere with work. Some of the main personal reasons for poor performance are:

Intellectual ability may be inappropriate for the job. This may be due to poor selection, changes over time whilst the person has been at work, or to the work having changed.

Emotional stability—or lack of it—makes it difficult to work with others or to work reliably. Again, this may be poor selection but often it is the result of a change. The difficult question is often how permanent is the emotional state.

Physical ability may be inappropriate for the work. This may change with age, for example the need for reading glasses is quite common. But often there are changes in the job.

Health. Poor health often makes people unreliable. Sometimes there is a permanent deterioration in their physical ability such that they can no longer cope with a full day's work.

Domestic circumstances. Problems with child care, elderly parents, spouse, etc., can all affect people's work. So can the physical aspects of domestic life such as the car not starting. The problem of two-career families is one that many organizations are increasingly having to face when managers refuse to relocate.

Family break-up in the medium term can make work difficult. As well as the obvious emotional aspects the employee involved may have money and housing worries.

Organizational characteristics

Aspects of the organization that are outside an individual's control can lead to their performing badly. Usually it is because the work is in some way not suitably organized. This may be resolved by new or clearer instructions and training or a rethink about the job itself. Sometimes it is necessary to transfer the individual to other work in the organization. Areas to consider are given below.

Assignment and job. Sometimes individuals simply do not know what is expected of them. They may have been away when new instructions were given, or have arrived recently. The job may be impossible for one person to do or so badly thought out that it is only possible to do it in this 'poor' way.

Job changed. The actual work that people do may be changed by new technology, practice or products. In addition the whole job may be reorganized to fit in with new ideas about the department or section. Where this does not make sense to the individual because of lack of communication or disagreement they are less likely to work well.

Pay. If the pay is felt to be too low, then the work is likely to suffer. If there is a felt unfairness it is likely to affect the work done. The poor administration of pay, such as late payment, wrong deductions, etc., can make people less willing to contribute their best.

Investment in equipment. Although we say, 'A poor workman always blames his tools,' there is very little a worker can do if there are not enough of the right materials and tools to work with.

Physical conditions. If people are hot, cold, wet, hungry, tired, deafened, cramped or in some other way irritated or made uncomfortable by their environment they will be distracted from work.

Location and transport. When companies relocate there are obvious implications for the employees. Sometimes employees feel it has been a deliberate ploy by management to test loyalty and reduce manpower. Reorganization of shifts and working hours can lead to problems where public transport timetables have not been considered.

Planning. Poor work can result from lack of suitable plans. The plans may be too idealistic, too constrained, out of touch with reality, too few or out of date. With planning goes some degree of improvization. This may have become too frequent, or not frequent enough, so the individual does not know what they are trying to do.

Training. There may be difficulties if the wrong training has been given, or the training has been given in the wrong way, if there has not been enough training or it is out of date.

Discipline. Different groups develop their own rules about what is regarded as appropriate behaviour. When a group normally runs on self-discipline there may not be enough formal processes to tell the poor performer about her work. There may be inappropriate permissiveness. Equally incompatible is the person in another group who finds they are irritated by the strict procedures being used for small errors.

Management. There may be poor management. There may be a particular manager, such as the person's immediate boss, who has not acted appropriately. It may be the management system as a whole that is causing problems, such as when managers spend more time being managers than getting on with the job of management.

Individual characteristics

Individual reasons for problem performance arise from a mismatch between the individual and the organization. It may be just a mismatch with the particular working group, or the individual may not fit into the organization. Some cases can be dealt with by tackling the particular issue, others by moving the person to another group, but some may necessitate moving the individual from the organization if things get too bad. Some of the more common reasons for this happening are:

Group dynamics. It may be that the person concerned does not fit in with the group and has become the butt of complaints. It may be that even if their work is adequate the rest of the group will not believe it. A self-fulfilling prophecy may be at work.

Personality clash – either with the boss or within the group – is more frequently given as a reason than is probably appropriate. Giving this reason rather suggests that nothing can be done about it. It is always worth asking whether anything else could also be affecting the situation.

Sense of fair play abused. This can occur when there are different views of the 'right way to do or say things'. It may just be because of some particular incident such as a promotion. It may be a general feeling, such as 'I don't like the way management speak to us.'

Conflict of religious or moral values. Someone may be asked to do something which is morally repugnant to them, and so they refuse to do it. Colleagues may feel they abuse this argument.

Inappropriate levels of confidence. The over-confident person who keeps getting things wrong is just as frustrating as the under-confident person who will not try anything new. Both types are familiar problems that require all the personal skills of the manager. Training and coaching may assist.

Motivation. We say someone is not motivated when we cannot think of any other good reason for their apparent lack of interest in their work. It may genuinely be the case that they are not sufficiently excited by the job, or the rewards it brings, to make a suitable contribution, but often some other reason can explain poor work.

Poor understanding of the job. This comes about when efforts made both by the individual and by the organization to communicate about the work required still do not manage to inculcate a suitable understanding of what is required or how to achieve it. All the difficulties of communication from sender to receiver (see chapter 7) could be at fault here.

Having established the gap in performance and found the reasons for it, we are in a better position to do something about it.

Dealing with the problem person

The two stages of identifying a gap and finding the reasons for that gap are important only in so far as they serve the main purpose of dealing with the poor performance, that is, improving it. Having established the reason or reasons for the poor performance, some starting points for doing something about it will suggest themselves. (See figure 25.) But, whatever the starting point, there always needs first to be a discussion with the problem person.

Counselling

The discussion may take place in an appraisal, disciplinary or other interview. The important point is to ensure that after the historical review of past performance the interview moves on to

Figure 25
Ways of dealing with the poor performer

The following are not given in order of execution but as
starting points to assist thinking when a problem arises.

Goal setting. Jointly agree specific, reasonable goals, and a
date to review the performance.

Training. Make sure you give appropriate training, preferably
on the job, so there is no problem in making the connection
between the training and the working situation.

Dissatisfactions. Fill the gap where appropriate; remedy
particular problems such as pay or conditions.

Discipline. These range from the informal discussion through
to increasingly formal procedures and punishment
ultimately including dismissal.

Reorganizing. Where the problem has arisen through
difficulties with the work materials, reporting relationships;
physical arrangements being no longer adequately
organized.

Management. Improve the clarity of communicating the task,
monitoring systems or the expertise of a particular manager.

Outside agencies. Particularly appropriate where there are
personal and family reasons.

The job. Transfer to a more appropriate job or department;
redesign the job.

Peer pressure. Where an individual performance is very
different from the average, those working alongside will feel
it inappropriate and may put pressure on the individual to
change.

Source: D. Torrington *and* J. Weightman, *Action Management*, London,
Institute of Personnel Management, 1991.

looking ahead to future performance. As neither the manager nor
the problem person knows the whole answer before the interview
starts, some sort of joint problem-solving and goal-setting is
required. These jointly agreed, specific, reasonable goals need

to be written down, with an agreed date for a review of the performance.

Counselling is not the same as giving advice. It is part of the manager's art to enable other people to develop their skills and effectiveness by helping them to find solutions to problems and develop strengths of their own. The role of the counsellor is to provide a different perspective in which to try ideas out. Those being counselled need to find their own solutions and exercise their own responsibility. Neither the counsellor nor the problem person knows the 'answer' before the interview begins; it emerges from the process itself.

This process can be effective only if the counsellor is willing to listen. Listening requires more than just allowing the other person to talk. There must be a willingness to believe that the other person has something to say and making sure you have understood it rather than making assumptions from your own point of view. This requires the counsellor to pay attention to the other and not be distracted. It needs to be clear that there is plenty of time for the discussion, with no furtive glances at the watch. The meeting needs to be private and free from interruption.

The style, warmth, integrity and authority of the counsellor are going to be the key to how effective the process is. There are some sequences that seem to suit several people: one is shown in figure 26.

Counselling is not just about 'healing the patient,' it is also about getting people to perform better so that they can contribute effectively to the work process. By finding a genuine solution to the reasons for poor work there is a better chance of the solution being permanent.

Other strategies

After the initial interview with the poor performer you may need to involve other people in changing things. If the reasons for the poor performance are largely due to *personal characteristics* it is best to inform the personnel department. They will know how to contact outside agencies who can help with the particular issue. They may well have someone dealing specifically with welfare. There are probably company guidelines on how long to persevere with personal problems. It is also important to advise the personnel

Figure 26
Stages in a counselling interview

1. *Factual interchange* Focus on the facts of the situation first. Ask factual questions and provide factual information, like the doctor asking about the location of the pain and other symptoms, rather than demonstrating dismay. This provides a basis for later analysis.

2. *Opinion interchange* Open the matter up for discussion by asking for the client's opinions and feelings, but not offering any criticism, nor making any decisions. Gradually, the matter is better understood by both counsellor and client.

3. *Joint problem-solving* Ask the client to analyze the situation described. The client will receive help from the counsellor in questioning and focus, but it must be the client's own analysis, with the counsellor resisting the temptation to produce answers.

4. *Decision-making* The counsellor helps to generate alternative lines of action for the client to consider and they both share in deciding what to do. Only the client can behave differently, but the counsellor may be able to help a change in behaviour by facilitation.

Source: D. Torrington *and* J. Weightman, *Action Management*, London, Institute of Personnel Management, 1991.

department, as there needs to be feedback to the recruitment process should it have proved inappropriate.

If the reasons for the poor performance are largely due to aspects of *organization* there are various strategies. Some of the problems may be because you have not managed suitably and some changes are necessary, in the way you assign jobs, plan, train, discipline and invest in equipment. By the time you have completed this book it is to be hoped that it will be less likely, but none of us ever gets everything right! You may also need to involve others in the changes in the organization of the work. Your boss and the personnel department would most likely be the first people to talk to.

When poor performance is due largely to *individual* reasons there are a variety of strategies to consider. The previous chapter may help with ways of getting performance from individuals.

You may want to consult the personnel department about idiosyncratic behaviour or beliefs. You might involve other members of the group and induce them to be more tolerant or encouraging of the particular individual.

Discipline and dismissal

All the previous sections have been about disciplining, in the sense of trying to change someone's performance, but at some point a manager may feel that the process needs to be more formal. It is, however, advisable to keep records of what has happened from the earliest stages just in case things get to the point of formal procedures.

Most organizations will have procedures for discipline and dismissal. The personnel department and trade union representatives will know them in detail. It is worth consulting them to ensure that you follow them. Many employers use the ACAS code of practice as the basis of their procedures.[2] ACAS have also published an advisory booklet, *Discipline at Work*.[3] Figure 27 shows the ACAS checklist for handling a disciplinary matter. There are several areas that may lead to discipline procedures besides poor performance, e.g. where rules necessary to maintain standards have been broken—such as in absence, health and safety, misconduct, the use of company facilities, timekeeping and holiday arrangements.

When all the above ideas, and no doubt lots of others as well, have been tried but have failed to improve performance, there comes a point when a decision to dismiss the problem person has to be faced. It is important that, where this is a possible outcome, procedure is closely adhered to. The legislation on unfair dismissal is clear. You are advised not to dismiss an employee without involving Personnel or some other manager.

Implications for managers

Managing the individual who has been performing badly over a long period of time is amongst the most difficult management tasks. There are no easy solutions. It is worth trying to fathom out why it is they have performed so badly, as the exercise will suggest solutions. To say, 'They are poorly motivated,' or 'There is a

Figure 27
Checklist for handling a disciplinary matter

1. Gather all the relevant facts: promptly, before memories fade, take statements, collect documents, in serious cases consider suspension with pay while an investigation is conducted.

2. Be clear about the complaint: is action needed at this stage?

3. If so, decide whether the action should be:
   - advice and counselling
   - formal disciplinary action.

4. If formal action is required, arrange a disciplinary interview:
   - ensure that the individual is aware of the nature of the complaint and that the interview is a disciplinary one
   - tell the individual where and when the interview will take place and of a right to be accompanied
   - try to arrange for a second member of management to be present.

5. Start by introducing:
   - those present and the purpose of the interview
   - the nature of the complaint
   - the supporting evidence.

6. Allow the individual to state his/her case:
   - consider and question any explanations put forward.

7. If any new facts emerge:
   - decide whether further investigation is required
   - if it is, adjourn the interview and reconvene when the investigation is completed.

8. Except in very straightforward cases, call an adjournment before reaching a decision:
   - come to a clear view about the facts

   - if they are disputed, decide on the balance of probability what version of the facts is true.

9. Before deciding the penalty consider:
   - the gravity of the offence and whether the procedure gives guidance
   - the penalty applied in similar cases in the past
   - the individual's disciplinary record and general service
   - any mitigating circumstances
   - whether the proposed penalty is reasonable in all the circumstances.

10 Reconvene the disciplinary interview to:
   - clearly inform the individual of the decision and the penalty, if any
   - explain the right of appeal and how it operates
   - in the case of a warning, explain what improvement is expected, how long the warning will last and what the consequences of failure to improve may be.

11. Record the action taken:
   - if other than an oral warning, confirm the disciplinary action to the individual in writing
   - keep a simple record of the action taken for future reference.

12. Monitor the individual's performance:
   - disciplinary action should be followed up, with the object of encouraging improvement
   - monitor progress regularly and discuss it with the individual.

Source: ACAS, *Discipline at work*, London, ACAS, 1987.

personality clash,' is only the starting point for analysis. Why are they poorly motivated? Why is there a clash of personalities? Once a reason or reasons become clear it is worth sitting down and talking to the individual concerned. They too may have been worrying about their performance. It is also worth seeking help from Personnel or your boss to talk about strategies for managing the problem. The Video Arts film *I'd like a word with you* is very popular for training in this area. The same company's book on management, produced from the films, is also worth looking at.[4]

Summary statements for managers

- The long-term poor performer is the most difficult person to deal with.
- The sequence for tackling the problem is: establish a gap in performance, establish the reasons for the gap; do something about it.
- Poor performance is due to personal, organizational or individual factors.
- A problem-solving interview with the person concerned is recommended.
- Discipline and dismissal both have associated procedures.

References

1   For further discussion of these see J. B. MINER and J. F. BREWER, 'The management of ineffective performance', in *Handbook of industrial and organizational psychology*, ed. M. D. Dunnette. Chicago, Rand McNally, 1976, and V. and A. STEWART, *Managing the poor performer*. Aldershot, Gower, 1982.
2   Advisory Conciliation and Arbitration Service, *Code of practice: disciplinary practice and procedures in employment*. Available free from ACAS or HMSO, London, 1977.
3   Advisory Conciliation and Arbitration Service, *Discipline at work*. Available free from ACAS, London, 1987.
4   Video Arts, *So you think you can manage?* London, Methuen, 1984.

Glossary

Adaptive Appropriate for the person, place or situation.

Alienation The separation of people from important decisions, other people and outcomes.

Attitudes An individual's orientation towards people, events and activities that are derived from their beliefs and experiences.

Authority Being able to influence things: *in* authority relies on position; *an* authority is based on expertise.

Communication Used in organizations to cover a wide range of behaviours and situations: to organize, to exchange information, to influence etc.

Concrete experience *Doing* something rather than talking about it.

Core employees The permanent, usually full-time, employees on whom the organization depends to perform its key functions who are likely to receive greater opportunities for training and development.

Credibility Used in organizations to refer to people who are worthy of belief, trustworthy, respected and convincing.

Culture The characteristic values and beliefs of an organization seen in the way people treat each other.

Dysfunctional Counter-productive or unhelpful.

Equal opportunity Ensuring that all people, regardless of race, gender, religious belief, disability etc. have similar access to selection, training, promotion, conditions of service etc.

Feedback Giving information and opinion about the performance to the performer.

Functional Helps to make something work or person develop.

Gender Male and female.

Generalization Applying a behaviour or concept to other examples.

Groups A collection of people who set a boundary between themselves and others, take decisions and delegate authority amongst themselves.

Human resource management Managing the people at work.

Maladaptive Not appropriate for the person or situation.

Morale The overall feeling amongst employees within a section, department or organization.

Motivation The inner drives and needs that we presume make people work for some things and not others.

Networks Personal connections with people who can be consulted, talked to and relied on for information, resources and help.

Perception The process of selecting, organizing and interpreting incoming stimulation.

Peripheral workers Temporary or contract employees (often part-time) who may have less job security than core employees.

Personality theories Different ways of analyzing and accounting for the differences between people.

Personnel Management Is concerned with managing the employment relationship; it is done by all managers as well as by specialist departments.

Psychology The study of behaviour, including descriptions and analyses of particular behaviours.

Recruitment Covers the whole process of acquiring people whose skills match the organization's needs: identifying job vacancies, attracting and assessing candidates, placement and follow up.

Selection Part of the recruitment procedure which assesses the candidates to reach a decision.

Sociology The study of society and its effect on its members.

Stress Being under pressure which can lead to physical and mental disorders.

Teams Individuals working together, whose collective performance is most effective in achieving the task.

Bibliography

ADVISORY CONCILIATION AND ARBITRATION SERVICE. *Code of practice*. I. *Disciplinary practice and procedures in employment*. London, HMSO, 1977.

ADVISORY CONCILIATION AND ARBITRATION SERVICE. *Workplace communications*. London, ACAS, 1985.

ADVISORY CONCILIATION AND ARBITRATION SERVICE. *Recruitment and selection*. Advisory Booklet No. 6. London, ACAS, 1986.

ADVISORY CONCILIATION AND ARBITRATION SERVICE. *Discipline at work*. London, ACAS, 1987.

ALBAN-METCALFE, B., and NICHOLSON, N. *The career development of British managers*, London, British Institute of Management, 1984.

ANTHONY, P. D. *The ideology of work*. London, Tavistock Publications, 1977.

ANTHONY, P. D. *The foundation of management*. Tavistock Publications, London, 1986.

ARGYRIS, C., and SCHÖN, D. *Organizational learning*. Reading, Mass., Addison-Wesley, 1978.

ARMSTRONG, M. *Management processes and functions*. London, Institute of Personnel Management, 1990.

BALES, R. F. *Interaction process analysis*. Reading, Mass., Addison-Wesley, 1950.

BANDURA, A. *Social learning theory*. Hemel Hempstead, Prentice Hall, 1977.

BELBIN, E. and R. M. *Problems in adult retraining*. London, Heinemann, 1972.

BELBIN, R. M. *Management teams: why they succeed or fail*. London, Heinemann, 1981.

BEYNON, H. *Working for Ford*. Harmondsworth, Penguin Books, 1973.

BLAUNER, R. *Alienation and freedom: the factory worker and his industry*. Chicago, University of Chicago Press, 1967.

BOYATZIS, R. E. *The competent manager: a model for effective performance*. Chichester, Wiley, 1982.

BRITISH INSTITUTE OF MANAGEMENT. *The responsive organization*. London, BIM, 1989.

BUZAN, A. *How to make the most of your mind*. London, Colt Books, 1977.

CARTER, A. *Authority and democracy*. London, Allen & Unwin, 1979.

CARTWRIGHT, D., and ZANDER, A. *Group dynamics*, third edition. London, Tavistock Publications, 1968.

165

CASEY, D. 'When is a team not a team?' *Personnel Management*, January 1985, pp. 26–9.

DAHL, R. *Modern political analysis*, second edition. Englewood Cliffs, N.J., Prentice Hall, 1970.

DAWSON, C. 'The moving frontiers of personnel management: human resource management or human resource accounting?' *Personnel Review*, 18, 3, 1989.

DICKSON, N. S. *The psychology of military incompetence*. London, Jonathan Cape, 1976.

EYSENCK, H. J. *The measurement of personality*. Lancaster, MTP Press, 1976.

FARNHAM, D. *The corporate environment*. London, Institute of Personnel Management, 1990.

FOX, A. *A sociology of work in industry*. London, Collier Macmillan, 1971.

FRASER, J. MUNROE. *Employment interviewing*. London, Macdonald & Evans, 1950.

FREUD, S. *Two short accounts of psychoanalysis*. Harmondsworth, Penguin Books, 1962.

FRIEDMAN, H., and MEREDEEN, S. *The dynamics of industrial conflict: lessons from Ford*. London, Croom Helm, 1980.

GAGNE, R. M. *Essentials of learning for instruction*. New York, Holt Rinehart & Winston, 1975.

GALE, J. *et al.*, 'Training methods compared', *Leadership and Organization Journal*, 1982, pp. 13–17.

GOLDTHORPE, J. H., LOCKWOOD, D., BECHHOFER, F., and PLATT, J. *The affluent worker in the class struggle*. Cambridge, Cambridge University Press, 1969.

GREENBAUM, H. W. 'The audit of organizational communications'. *Academy of Management Journal*, 1974, pp. 739–54.

HACKMAN, J. R. 'Work design', in *Motivation and work behaviour*, ed. R. M. Steers and L. W. Porter, fourth edition. London, McGraw-Hill, 1987.

HAMBLIN, A. *Evaluation and control of training*. London, McGraw-Hill, 1974.

HANDY, C. 'The organisations of consent', in *The changing university*, ed. D. Piper and R. Glatter. Windsor, National Foundation for Educational Research, 1977.

HANDY, C. *The future of work: a guide to changing society*. Oxford, Blackwell, 1984.

HANDY, C. *Understanding organizations*, second edition. Harmondsworth, Penguin Books, 1985.

HARVEY-JONES, J. *Making it happen: reflections on leadership*. London, Collins, 1988.

HERZBERG, F. 'One more time: how do you motivate employees?' *Harvard Business Review*, January-February 1968.

INDUSTRIAL TRAINING RESEARCH UNIT. *Choose an effective style: a self-instructional approach to the teaching of skills*. Cambridge, ITRU, 1976.

JANIS, I. L. *Victims of groupthink*. Boston, Mass., Houghton Mifflin, 1972.

KELLY, G. *The psychology of personal constructs*. New York, Norton, 1955.

KLINE, P. *Psychology exposed*. London, Routledge, 1989.

KOLB, D. A., RUBIN, I. M., and McINTYRE, J. M. *Organizational psychology: and experimental approach*. Englewood Cliffs, N.J., Prentice Hall, 1974.

KOTTER, J. *The general managers*. New York, Free Press, 1982.

LEAVITT, H. J. 'Some aspects of certain communication patterns on group performance'. *Journal of Abnormal and Social Psychology*, 45, 1951, pp. 38–50.

LEAVITT, H. J. *Managerial psychology*, fourth edition. Chicago, University of Chicago Press, 1978.

LEAVITT, H. J. *et al.*, *The organizational world*. New York, Harcourt Brace Jovanovich, 1973.

LEGGE, K. 'Human resource management: a critical analysis', in *New perspectives on human resource management*, ed. J. Storey. London, Routledge, 1988.

LEWIN, K. *Field theory in social science*, ed. D. Cartwright. London, Tavistock Publications, 1952.

LUTHANS, F., and KREITNER, R. *Organizational behavior modification*. Glenville, Ill., Scott Foresman, 1975.

McGREGOR, D. *The human side of enterprise*. New York, McGraw-Hill, 1960.

McMAHON, A., BOLEM, R., and HOLLY, P. *Guidelines for review and internal development in schools: primary/secondary school handbook GRIDS*. Schools Council Programme No. 1. York, Longman and Schools Council, 1984.

MANSFIELD, R., POOLE, M., BLYTON, P., and FROST, P., *The British manager in profile*. British Institute of Management Survey No. 51. London, BIM, 1981.

MARSH, P., BARWISE, P., THOMAS, K., and WENSLEY, R. *Managing strategic investment decisions in large diversified companies*. London, London Business School, 1988.

MARX, K. 'On alienation', in *Karl Marx: selected writings in sociology and social philosophy*. Harmondsworth, Penguin Books, 1963.

MASLOW, A. H. *Motivation and personality*. New York, Harper & Row, 1954.

MILLS, C. *White collar: the american middle classes*. New York, Oxford University Press, 1956.

MINER, J. B., and BREWER, J. F. 'The management of ineffective performance', in *Handbook of industrial and organizational psychology*, ed. M. D. Dunnette. Chicago, Rand McNally, 1976.

MORGAN, G. *Images of organization*. Beverly Hills, Cal., Sage Publications, 1986.

MUMFORD, E. 'Job satisfaction: a method of analysis'. *Personnel Review*, summer 1972.

NEISSER, U. *Cognitive psychology*. New York, Appleton-Century-Crofts, 1966.

PEDLER, M., BURGOYNE, J., and BOYDELL, T. *A manager's guide to self-development*, second edition. Maidenhead, McGraw-Hill, 1986.

PETERS, T. J., and WATERMAN, R. H. *In search of excellence.* London, Harper & Row, 1982.

PLUMBLEY, P. *Recruitment and selection*, fourth edition. London, Institute of Personnel Management, 1985.

REVANS, R. W. *Developing effective managers.* London, Longman, 1971.

RICE, A. K. *Productivity and social organisation.* London, Tavistock Publications, 1958.

RODGER, A. *The Seven-point Plan.* London, National Institute of Industrial Psychology, 1952.

ROGERS, C. R. *On becoming a person.* London, Constable, 1967.

SCHEIN, E. H. *Process consultation: its role in organization development.* Reading, Mass., Addison-Wesley, 1969.

SCHEIN, E. H. *Organizational psychology*, third edition. Englewood Cliffs, N.J., Prentice Hall, 1980.

SCHEIN, E. H. *Organizational culture and leadership.* San Francisco, Jossey Bass, 1985.

SCHUTZ, W. C. *The interpersonal world.* New York, Science and Behavior Books, 1966.

SKINNER, B. F. *Science and human behavior.* New York, Macmillan Free Press, 1953.

SLOBIN, D. I. *Psycholinguistics.* Glenville, Ill., Scott Foresman, 1971.

SMITH, M., BECK, J., COOPER, C., COX, C., OTTAWAY, D., and TALBOT, R., *Introducing organizational behaviour.* London, Macmillan, 1982.

STEERS, R. M., and PORTER, L. W. (eds.) *Motivation and work behaviour*, fourth edition. London, McGraw-Hill, 1987.

STEWART, R. *Choices for managers.* Maidenhead, McGraw-Hill, 1982.

STEWART, V. and A. *Managing the poor performer.* Aldershot, Gower, 1982.

TORRINGTON, D. P. *Face to face in management.* Hemel Hempstead, Prentice Hall, 1982.

TORRINGTON, D. P., and CHAPMAN, J. *Personnel management.* Hemel Hempstead, Prentice Hall, 1979.

TORRINGTON, D. P., and HALL, L. A. *Personnel management: a new approach.* Hemel Hempstead, Prentice Hall, 1987.

TORRINGTON, D. P., and WEIGHTMAN, J. B. 'Middle management work'. *Journal of General Management*, 1987.

TORRINGTON, D. P., and WEIGHTMAN, J. B. *Management and organisation in secondary schools: training materials.* Oxford, Blackwell, 1989.

TORRINGTON, D. P., WEIGHTMAN, J. B., and JOHNS, K. *Effective management: people and organization.* Hemel Hempstead, Prentice Hall, 1989.

TUCKMAN, B. W. 'Development sequences in small groups'. *Psychological Bulletin*, 63, 1965, pp. 384–99.

TYSON, S. 'The management of the personnel function'. *Journal of Management Studies*, 1987, pp. 523–32.

TYSON, S., and YORK, A. *Personnel management made simple.* London, Heinemann, 1982.

VIDEO ARTS. *So you think you can manage?* London, Methuen, 1984.

VROOM, V., and DECI, E. *Management and motivation*. London, Penguin Books, 1974.

WAGNER, R. F. 'The employment interview: a critical appraisal'. *Personnel Psychology*, 2, 1949, pp. 17–40.

WATSON, J. B. *Behaviourism*. Chicago, University of Chicago Press, 1924.

WATSON, T. *Sociology, work and industry*. London, Routledge, 1980.

WEBER, M. *The Protestant ethic and the spirit of capitalism*. London, Allen & Unwin, 1965.

WEICK, K. *The social psychology of organizing*. Reading, Mass., Addison-Wesley, 1979.

Index